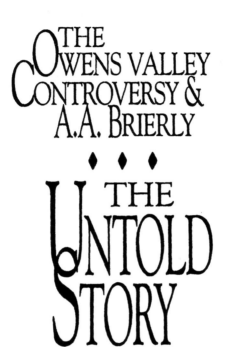

THE OWENS VALLEY CONTROVERSY & A.A. BRIERLY

♦ ♦ ♦

THE UNTOLD STORY

ROBERT A. PEARCE, Ph.D.

Dageforde Publishing, Inc.

ISBN: 1-886225-37-0

Cover art by Angie Johnson Art Productions

Library of Congress Cataloging-in-Publication Data

Pearce, Robert A. (Robert Alan), 1956-
    The Owens Valley controversy & A.A. Brierly : the untold story / Robert A. Pearce.
        p.   cm.
    ISBN 1-886225-37-0
    1. Owens River Valley (Calif.)--Social conditions.   2. Owens River Valley (Calif.)--History--20th century.   3. Water rights-
-California--Owens River Valley--History--20th century.   4. Water rights--Economic aspects--California--Owens River Valley.   5. Water -Supply--California--Owens River Valley--History--20th century.
    6. Brierly, A.A.   7. Owens River Valley (Calif.)--Water rights.
    8. Owens River Valley (Calif.)--Social conditions.   9. Los Angeles (Calif.). Dept. of Water and Power--History.   I. Title.
    II. Title: Owens Valley controversy and A.A. Brierly.
HN79.C220725   1999
306'.09794'9--dc21
                                            99-30722
                                            CIP

Dageforde Publishing, Inc.
122 South 29th Street
Lincoln, Nebraska 68510
Phone: (402) 475-1123   FAX: (402) 475-1176
Visit our Web Site at
http://www.dageforde.com

Printed in the United States of America
10   9   8   7   6   5   4   3   2   1

Contents

A.A. Brierly

To my grandfather "Pa,"
thank you for your guidance.
It was great to have an "80-year-old kid"
to play with. I wish we could hop in "Ole Dolly Dodge"
and head up Mazourka Canyon.

Acknowledgments

Thanks go to:

Betty Martinson who edited the manuscript before it went to press.

Arlene Pearce, my mom, who read this manuscript more than anyone and who provided needed corrections.

Bud Cashbaugh, who spent time with me reminiscing about how the Owens Valley was when he was young. I enjoyed our past conversations sitting under the willow trees next to the irrigation ditch on Warm Springs Road and I look forward to more of the same.

Wilfred Partridge, who gave me so much to think about. I will never forget the conversations about his youth in the Owens Valley, and his feelings about the DWP. I miss listening to Wilfred tell stories as we sat on his patio.

Charles Delameter for the use of his interview with my grandfather.

California

Inyo County

Bishop
Big Pine
Owens Valley Region
Independence
Lone Pine
Keeler
Olancha/Cartago
Tecopa

Sierra Nevada Mountains

Owens Valley is located on the western edge of Inyo County between the Sierra Nevada Mountains on the west and the Inyo and White Mountains on the east.

Introduction

Southern skies flame orange and red, the tips of jagged snow-capped peaks hide in the dark clouds of an oncoming storm, and a whispering, chilling breeze blows as I stand on what was once part of my family's ranch. I feel blessed to be part of such awe-inspiring natural wonder. No other land is as fascinating to me as the Owens Valley (the Valley) and surrounding mountains. Fall is *my* time of year in the Valley. Cottonwoods radiate beauty with their golden leaves; the air is crisp and makes one feel alive. It is the time of year when storms travel in and drop the beginnings of winter on the Sierra Nevada, White, and Inyo Mountains. It is truly a miracle that, amongst all this grandeur, the land is undeveloped and the presence of man minute. Time seems to stand still in Owens Valley. I thank the DWP* (Los Angeles Department of Water and Power) for what exists in the Valley.

---

* In referring to the Los Angeles Department of Water and Power, several terms are used interchangeably by locals in the Eastern Sierra Region: the City, DWP, Los Angeles, the Department, LA, all refer to the same agency.

I am the fifth generation of my family to live in Owens Valley, and thus my family and I have a long history in the region. How fortunate that I grew up with people, older generation family members and their friends, who were in the Valley when the city of Los Angeles began land purchases for the water rights to quench the thirst of southern California. Many of these people knew some of the original pioneers who settled the Valley, giving them first hand knowledge of what the Valley looked like prior to the turn of the twentieth century. I have become increasingly aware that these old-timers told a much different story of the events around the turn of the century and what the region's environment was like, than that which is currently being told by many individuals regarding the DWP and the Owens Valley. I feel it is important that the details I know of the land purchases and the Owens Valley's environment are told.

Some background information is warranted for those readers not familiar with the controversy involving the Los Angeles Department of Water and Power and the County of Inyo in eastern California.

The Eastern Sierra Region has several small communities including Independence, Olancha, and Big Pine, with populations around 1,000 people each. There are also two larger communities; Lone Pine (population 1,818) and Bishop (population 3,475). The area directly surrounding Bishop has about 11,000 people. These communities are all located in Inyo County which has a population of about 18,400.

Los Angeles began purchasing land from farmers and ranchers in the Owens Valley (Eastern Sierra Region of California) shortly after 1900. The purpose of the land acquisition was to obtain water rights and transport surface and groundwater to Los Angeles, a distance of about 200 miles. There are currently two aqueducts that leave the southern part of Owens Valley and transport water to Los Angeles. There have been several legal battles between Los Angeles and the County of Inyo over land management and water issues. The story was romanticized in the movie *Chinatown*. Currently, Los Angeles owns over 300,000 acres in the area and, in essence, controls the growth and development of that land. Much of the land is leased to ranchers and farmers for livestock production and alfalfa farming. The majority of the Los Angeles-owned lands in the region are open to the public for recreational use. One of the more well-known legal battles concerned DWP's water diversions from Mono Lake.

Recently, the County of Inyo and the Los Angeles Department of Water and Power finalized a Memorandum of Understanding (MOU) which incudes many agreements on how Los Angeles will manage water and land in the eastern Sierra. Included in the MOU are: land releases for development around each of the Owens Valley towns; rewatering of the Lower Owens River (water was diverted completely out of the river and into an aqueduct north of Independence for transport to Los Angeles); land releases for mitigation purposes; and development of management plans for leased ranch lands. There are about fifty miles of dry river channel that will be rewatered under the MOU.

The Los Angeles Department of Water and Power is also required to control dust produced from Owens Lake, now a dry lake bed. Water diversions by the Los Angeles Department of Water and Power and agricultural interests prior to Los Angeles purchasing land caused the lake to dry up. Land and water issues in the

Owens Valley related to Los Angeles are complex and politically explosive.

Much has been written and discussed which portrays Los Angeles as a "villain" who robbed the ranchers and farmers of their lands. Others talk about the environmental degradation caused by Los Angeles to the Eastern Sierra Region.

This story deals primarily with the Owens Valley (located in the Eastern Sierra Region) and my grandfather's involvement with land sales to Los Angeles. I've included my grandfather's views about Los Angeles, and how his views have shaped my own thoughts on the subject. My grandfather had a much different view from what is often heard today.

It has become popular to talk about how DWP stole the lands in Owens Valley. However, Abraham Hoffman, in his book *Vision of Villainy*, noted the following "...the DWP continued to buy out farms at about four times their assessed valuation" (Hoffman, 1981). I have heard numerous people speak of how irrigation water was cut off from farmers who did not sell to DWP. However, Remi Nadeau author of *Water Seekers* wrote: "It was such minority farmers [those attached to the land by ties stronger than money], selling against their will, who naturally held a real grievance against the Los Angeles invasion. Yet their hate was caused more by fear than actual harm; in cases where isolated ranchers did not sell, their full share of water was scrupulously delivered by the Los Angeles Water Department" (Nadeau, 1997). Also, much has been made about how the Watterson brothers were the representatives of the Owens Valley ranchers and how they tried to save the Valley. Read again the words of Abraham Hoffman: "At the same time, it should be noted, the Wattersons did not speak for all the valley residents, or even a large part of them. Their followers consisted mainly of townspeople, particularly Bishop residents— the property owners of the Owens Valley Irrigation District who didn't sell and "outside interests," such as absentee landholders who benefited from the stand taken by the Wattersons" (Hoffman, 1981). These issues and others are presented from my grandfather's views. The statements from Nadeau and Hoffman show that there are others who do not always accept the "popular" version of DWP and the Owens Valley story.

I worry about the future of the Owens Valley. So much of what is considered fact about land and natural resource issues in the Valley has been built on a foundation of myths. The results of litigation and the Memorandum of Understanding between the Los Angeles Department of Water and Power and Inyo County could greatly alter the Valley's look and feel. For example, land releases under the MOU could destroy the rural setting in the Valley through increased development, and, as some Valley residents desire, through development of light industry on the released lands. I'm afraid these changes might be detrimental to the Valley. Much has been said about the evils of DWP. Most make a good story; sadly, they are not altogether truthful.

The following pages include recollections, first-hand discussions with people from another generation and time, and my own thoughts on Owens Valley issues. Most of the individuals I talk about have long since left us. I wish they were here now as the discussions about the Valley continue to build in intensity. We need their knowledge and vision.

My 1974 paper on the DWP land purchases is included in its original form. The text is presented in the present tense as if my grandfather were still alive. I chose to leave it as it was. I did not want to change what is a first-hand description of events. The statements in this introduction and the conclusion are my opinions, based on what I have gleaned over many years of listening to native ranchers and "Owens Valley old-timers." I have a belief system that runs against the views some other individuals have when discussions about the DWP are held. But my views are based on first hand experiences, not revisionary historical accounts.

There is a brief biography of my grandfather in this book. It is important for you to understand his life and his character. Such knowledge will reinforce the truth of his story of the Owens Valley and DWP interactions portrayed in this book. One example of his extraordinary character and outstanding view on life was that he worked for the County of Inyo for sixty-five years, starting in 1905. That is right, sixty-five years! He retired at eighty-five years young (as he always said). What is even more astonishing is that he never received a county benefit package—no retirement, no health care—and during his nearly forty years as Inyo County Surveyor, he received no regular salary. With the work climate as it is today, such practices seem unimaginable. I believe, however, that he thought this was the way things should be. He was, in the truest sense of the word, a public servant. When looking through many of his books, it is apparent to me that he was greatly influenced by writings of the founding fathers of our country. He believed that one has the responsibility to take care of oneself and not to rely on the government for security. Maybe he felt a bit like what Benjamin Franklin expressed in the following:

> As every Freeman, to preserve his independence, (if he has not a sufficient Estate) ought to have some profession, calling, trade or farm, whereby he may honestly subsist, there can be no necessity for, nor use in, establishing offices of profit [referring to government offices]; the usual effects of which are dependence and servility, unbecoming freemen, in the possessors and expectants; faction, contention, corruption, and disorder among the people. Wherefore whenever an office, thro' increase of fees or otherwise, becomes so profitable as to occasion many to apply for it, the profits ought to be lessened by the Legislature (Franklin).

My grandfather's ideologies had an extreme influence on my older brother Hugh and me. When we were little kids, we spent most weekends and a great deal of the summer with him. My younger brother Mark (six years younger than I) did not spend as much time with our grandfather as Hugh and I did. Yet, he has good memories of our grandfather. He remembers the lunch trips to the Pines Cafe in Independence for noon-time milk shakes.

My grandfather never owned a television and only occasionally listened to the news on a radio. Instead, he was an avid reader with an extensive library and innumerable magazine subscriptions. He used to read to us in the evenings. My favorite times were when he would read from *A Library of Poetry and Song* printed in

1871 (Bryant, 1871). I remember verses such as the following:

"Bring forth the horse!"
—the horse was brought
In truth, he was a noble steed,
A Tartar of the Ukraine breed,
Who looked as though the speed of thought
were in his limbs.

Away! — away! My breath was gone,
I saw not where he hurried on;
Twas scarcely yet the break of day,
And on he foamed, —away! —away!
                    Mazeppa's Ride, Byron

and:

I don't go much on religion;
I never ain't had no show;
But I've got a middlin' tight grip, sir,
On the handful o' things I know.
                    Little Breeches, John Hay

He also had many sayings, only a few of which I can recollect. I wish I had listened more intently to rhymes such as the following:

The saddest sight in the world of sin
is a little lost pup with his tail tucked in.
                    Title and Author Unknown

and

There came to my window one morning in spring
A sweet little robin, she came there to sing.
The songs that she sang were lovelier by far,

than ever were played on flute or guitar.
But just as she finished her beautiful song,
a thoughtless young man with a gun came along.
He killed and he carried my robin away,
no more will she sing at the breaking of day.
                                    Title and Author Unknown.

I first remember hearing these readings and recitations about the time I was seven or eight years old. My grandfather would read and talk to me for hours. Other times we would just wander through the musty pages of his books. His reading to me instilled a sense of inquisitiveness and a love for knowledge in me that has remained all my life.

Sometimes he would tell "old time stories." He could go on indefinitely. I never tired of them. He was the consummate storyteller. He filled my mind with tales of people like Giles and Thorpe—two miners who worked claims in Mazourka Canyon. He loved to discuss outlaws of the old west like Joaquin Murrieta, Sontag and Evans, Vasquez, and others. I remember his recollections about old-timers from his youth. He told their stories of Owens Valley towns like Bend City, San Carlos, Crisopolis, and Kearsarge City. These communities are all gone, but my grandfather knew people who were familiar with the old towns. His accounts of his youth and family kept our undivided attention and developed a desire in me to understand and "know" the Owens Valley. His stories and the time he spent with me fostered a deep love for Inyo County and the Owens Valley.

Another honorable characteristic of my grandfather is that when he was telling his "old-time stories" and he couldn't remember some particular point, he would say so. He didn't make things up to make the story good. I know other people whose reminiscences are more like "big windys" than historical recollection. My grandfather never fell into that trap. If he couldn't remember something, he said so and went on with the story.

During visits to his home in Independence, we would explore the Valley in his old 1950 Dodge pickup (Dolly Dodge). I was driving that old truck long before I ever had a license. I guess that is what was so different about him. He treated all kids as equals. Whether he was letting us drive at twelve or thirteen years old, reading poetry, or discussing the consequences of the unyielding human demands on natural resources (long before the topic was in vogue), he treated us with respect. There were lots of times I may not have grasped the full intent of his conversation; however, I now know that I learned more than I might have imagined. It is his strong influence that has, in part, shaped my views on the Valley.

Along with my grandfather, his generation of friends also influenced and shaped my understanding of the Valley. People like Garf Goodale, Richie Conway, Gus Cashbaugh, Frank Lawrence, Pete Mairs, and Lee Warlie, all locals born prior to or near 1900, frequently visited my grandfather. Many of these pioneer families are the namesakes for local sites. Goodale Creek, Goodale Peak, and Conway Summit received their names in recognition of these pioneer families. Though I didn't always pay strict attention to their conversations, I must have absorbed a lot because I remember so much.

Lee Warlie, a Paiute, worked for my grandfather on the family ranch for more than forty years. I never knew a man with more dignity and honor than Lee. When I was a kid, I used to sit with Lee in his pickup under a locust grove on our ranch. There he would recite Native American stories like the creation of the Paiute People. Lee would tell his stories in English and in his own Paiute language. Sometimes George Brown would come by, and he and Lee would converse in Paiute. They used to talk about the Valley and what life was like when they were young. I listened and I remember. These men are no longer around and the same experiences cannot be gathered today. I was very fortunate to have tasted their wisdom!

Another common characteristic of most of these men is that they came from simple beginnings. Though they weren't wealthy, they had comfortable lives in their old age. These men grew up without luxuries such as indoor plumbing and insulated houses. Much of what they needed to eat they raised or traded for. The same was true for many other basic necessities of life. They lived in a time when horses were the main means of travel. Many things we take for granted today were not available to these men when they were young. This type of life shaped and built unusual character in them. I believe most people today, including me, can not relate to the strife poor people living around the turn of the century faced. My grandfather talked about the snow blowing through the skeleton keyhole in the door and piling up on the floor of his childhood home. He lived in a board and batten building with a canvas ceiling for part of his youth. When he was young, there was no electricity or running water, and yet he lived to see men land on the moon. So, in his life, and in the lives of people in his generation, there was a wide range of experiences to which my generation (and those close to mine) cannot relate. Again, I realize how fortunate I was to be influenced by such individuals.

The point is that I have been profoundly inspired by a generation of people who were in this Valley prior to the presence of DWP. Therefore, my views are much different from some of today's political activists who wish to see less influence by DWP within the Valley. I hope my view will prevail.

It is my desire that the story contained in this book on the DWP land purchases will initiate a self-examination in those who hope to open the Valley up to development and private ownership. I believe such proposed changes will destroy the very thing that draws us to the Owens Valley in the first place. I am sometimes dismayed as I look to the south and see smog creeping in from southern California, or face the incessant stream of headlights coming from the south, or see the piles of trash along the banks of the Owens River. I hope the Valley can absorb all that is asked of its resources, and that we can keep the Valley unique and not follow actions of other regions. Let us not allow over-development and uncontrolled growth. We must not let economic development destroy the open spaces and natural beauty.

It is true, many people who wish to live in Owens Valley can't because of the lack of jobs and the high cost of living. However, I can't live in Yosemite National Park either. Yosemite is a place worth preserving, as is the Owens Valley. Though the grandeur is different between the two regions, the Owens Valley possesses its unique characteristics that must be preserved. We, as a society, must make choices to save some rural areas and keep them safe from development. There are those who will think my views are selfish and self-serving. However, for the long term, I know it is better to maintain the Valley as it is, as opposed to developing the land. The Owens Valley deserves to remain an open and, as much as possible, an unsettled region.

My Grandfather's Roots

My family called my grandfather "Pa." As a little boy, my brother Hugh came up with the "Pa" title. For this biography I'll call my grandfather by that name. Whether dressed in one of his custom-tailored suits, or decked out in Levis with the pant cuffs turned up and a flannel shirt, there were some things about my grandfather that never changed: the ever-present Stetson Open Road hat with the front brim turned slightly down; made-to-measure high-top Tony Lama black cowboy boots with underslung heels; and a constant trail of smoke from House of Delmage cigars. Pa never went without suspenders, and somewhere in his outfit was a red bandanna. For a young boy there was no better person to be with.

Much of the following life story was gleaned from a biography written by the Daughters of the American Revolution, from family history written by Pa, and from my mother. My grandfather spent many hours writing about his family. The family history portion of Pa's biography is condensed to give a feeling of our family's presence in this country and how we got to Owens Valley.

My grandfather, Arlington Austin Brierly, was known to his friends as "Arlie." He was born January 20, 1884, to Washington "Wash" Cassius Brierly and Rachel Enloe Brierly, just south of Bishop, California. The house was located east of where the Inyo County Maintenance yard is now, on south Main Street. His mother came to Inyo County on May 2, 1876, with her parents Hugh and

Enoch Enloe, late 1800s. The first person of the author's family to visit Owens Valley. He came through the Eastern Sierra in 1859 with a herd of cattle in route to the Mono Diggins.

Emily Enloe, three siblings, and four cousins. Emily Enloe had a sister who was already living in Bishop. Pa was raised around this large and close family. He always spoke fondly of his childhood days, and especially of his own grandfather, Hugh S. Enloe.

The first of my family to come to Owens Valley was Pa's uncle Enoch Enloe (named after Pa's great-great-grandfather), who, at the age of twelve in 1859, helped drive a herd of cattle through the Owens Valley en route to "Mono Diggings." After the trip, he returned home to the San Joaquin Valley. In any event, some of my family has been associated with the Valley for nearly 140 years.

Pa's maternal great-great-grandfather Enoch Enloe and Enoch's brother Isaac came to Maryland from Scotland in 1750. Both Enoch and Isaac fought in the American Revolution. From Maryland, the two brothers moved with their families to South Carolina. Enoch was married twice. His first wife died, and he remarried Jane McCord, Pa's great-great-grandmother. James Enloe, a son of Enoch's, was Pa's great-grandfather. James moved from South Carolina to Tennessee in 1808 and, in 1813, married Nancy Simpson (Pa's great-grandmother). From Tennessee, James went to Kentucky.

Pa's grandfather, Hugh Simpson Enloe, was born in either Kentucky or Tennessee. He did not know for sure because the family was moving when Hugh was born. From Kentucky, the Enloe family moved to Missouri. James and Nancy Enloe had thirteen children born between 1813 and 1836. Pa's maternal grandparents (my great-great-grandparents) came across the plains from Missouri in five months and five days with a wagon, and arrived in Jackson, Amador County, California, September 15, 1853. His mother, Rachel (my great-grandmother), was born three days later on September 18, 1853. Rachel was a member of the Covered Wagon Babies of America, a group of individuals who were born on the trip or made the trip across the plains in their mothers' wombs.

From stories my grandfather told, his mother was a remarkable woman who ran the family ranch while Wash (my great-grandfather) was off working in other parts of the state. Pa told how his mother secured a new clock when the family needed one. A jeweler in Bishop named R.W. Scott had a clock that would do just fine. She traded hay with the jeweler for the clock. However, Mr. Scott didn't need the hay right at that moment, so Pa's mother kept the hay. The only problem was when Mr. Scott decided he needed hay, Rachel didn't have any to give him. The Brierly's next door neighbor did have some hay. Pa's grandfather had some dried peaches, which Rachel traded with the neighbor for the hay to pay for the clock. My mother still has the clock. When reading the diaries of my great-great-grandfather (Hugh Enloe), it is very apparent that bartering was a common practice for obtaining all kinds of wares.

Hugh Enloe and his wife Emily (the author's great-great-grandparents). Taken at Bishop, California about 1890 or 1891.

Rachel had over 320 acres within two miles of Bishop at one time. Several crops, including alfalfa, wheat, and corn, were raised on the ranch. Pa said the land wasn't very productive, but the family grew enough to get by on. Pa's grandfather also had a ten-acre orchard and eighty acres of Rachel's land that was planted in orchards and alfalfa.

Pa's father, Wash, was six years old in 1853 when he left Iowa with his family bound for California. The wagon train his family was with left late in the year, making it only as far as Salt Lake City, Utah, where they spent the winter before traveling on to Jackson, California. Wash spent his youth in Amador County, Sacramento, and San Luis Obispo, California. He also spent some time in the Mineral King area on the west side of the Sierra Nevada Mountains. In 1863, at sixteen, Wash moved to Virginia City, Nevada, crossing the Sierra Nevada Mountains on snow shoes. He returned home to Amador County after a short time, later moving to Dayton, Nevada. In the late 1870s, while in Dayton, Wash heard of a gold strike in Mammoth Lakes, California, and moved to Mammoth.

Wash came to Bishop in the spring of 1881. In that same year, he met Rachel Enloe whom he married on July 17, 1881. My grandfather was born three years later. His sister Emily was born in 1891. Rachel and Wash also had a boy, Elwyn, who died in infancy. Rachel was Wash's second wife. His first wife, Carrie Austin, died of consumption (tuberculosis).

Pa's middle name came from his father's first wife's maiden name. Carrie and Wash had three chil-

The home in which A.A. Brierly grew up, located near Bishop, California. Taken in the late 1800s.

Taken in 1898. The Brierly family on its way to Yosemite for a vacation.
They traveled from Bishop to Yosemite with the outfit in this picture.
From left to right, Wash Brierly (author's great-grandfather), Rachel
Brierly (author's great-grandmother—notice the dog in her lap),
on the mule is A. A. Brierly and his sister Emily
(author's grandfather and great-aunt).

dren, Lorinda (died at three years old), Eliza (died at ten months of age), and Elsie (died as a little girl).

Wash's life was not easy. His father, Samuel Valentine Brierly, left him when he was seven. He took two of Wash's older brothers Isaac and Marshall and went back east. Later, Isaac served in the Confederate Army, while Marshall served with the North (at the battle of Pea Ridge, Arkansas, and at Shiloh, the brothers were in opposing armies!). When Samuel went back east, he left his wife, Wash, and three of Wash's sisters. As an adult, Wash lost a wife and four children. Times were hard for a good part of Wash's life.

Pa graduated from the grammar school system in Bishop. In those days, students shared desks (two students to a desk). His desk mate for the majority of his grammar school years was another old-timer, "Gus" Cashbaugh. Gus and Pa were just a few months apart in age and remained close friends throughout their lives. Grammar school life was much different from today. Pa told us how students would bring guns to school to hunt during lunch hours, and how many rode horses to and from school. After grammar school graduation Pa went to high school in Los Angeles.

The trip to Los Angeles was quite an undertaking in the early 1900s. The choice was to take a horse or a horse-drawn vehicle all the way to Los Angeles, or take the narrow gauge train to Keeler, a horse-drawn stage to Mojave, and then the train from there to the southland. The wagon trip could last as long as eleven days or more. On one of his first trips (horse drawn buggy) to Los Angeles, Pa and his father camped along the Los Angeles River. While they were out one day, someone stole a shotgun (used for hunting) and some other personal items. However, the thief left behind his own items, including a hair brush that Pa kept all his life.

While going to high school, Pa held a variety of jobs, including pulling nails from lumber at a demolition site, janitorial work at night for the high school, and loading freight into railroad box cars. His mother made all his shirts for him, as the family was very poor. The expense of high school must have been a burden on his family. At the same time, his enrollment at Los Angeles High School was a· significant achievement for him and his family. After graduation in 1905, Pa returned to Owens Valley to begin his sixty-five-year employment with the County of Inyo and to continue his ranching interests.

His first job as a teacher in Independence began on September 2, 1905. He also taught at the Reward Mine,

Laws, Warm Springs, Valley, Fort Independence, and West Bishop schools, for a total of fifteen years. There were many school districts in the early part of the century in the Owens Valley. Many of these schools were small one-room buildings with the teacher instructing all grade levels. Pa's first teaching position covered six grades and thirty-one pupils.

When Pa began teaching in Independence, the school was located on Jackson Street east of where the Courthouse now stands. Pa was twenty-one years old and was anxious as he began his new teaching position. He wasn't much older than some of his students. Many were strong young farm boys. In the class of sixteen girls and fifteen boys, there was a six-foot-four-

A. A. Brierly with his first group of students at the Independence Schoolhouse. Mr. Brierly is located in the doorway. Notice the 6'4" student on the left (One of the Lawrence boys). The author's grandmother was a student in the class. The author has names of some of the other students, too. Taken in 1905.

inch strapping farm boy (one of the Lawrence boys). Pa said "I was glad he was a good boy." Classes ran from 9 A.M. to 4 P.M. covering reading, penmanship, arithmetic, spelling, grammar, history, and geography. Pa received $30 a month, plus room and board at the Norman House (Market and Edwards Street) owned and operated by the Mairs family. Since the boarding house had no tub, baths were taken at Max Fausel's barber shop.

A. A. Brierly (at right, age 16) with his father, Wash Brierly. Taken in Los Angeles, California, 1900.

Pa told of a time when he had some trouble with a group of young students. In those days, paddling was still allowed. He had all the "trouble" students line up facing the class. Then Pa got behind them, told them all to bend forward, took two books, and began to bang them together. All of the students in the line-up thought they were going to be paddled and began sobbing at the sound of the books banging together (they thought someone was getting hit each time Pa hit the books together). The laughter from the rest of the class made more of an impression than actual paddling ever would have.

One of the most important memories I have of Pa is that he never got mad at my older brother or me, no

The Laws School class in 1909. A. A. Brierly is standiing in the righthand doorway. The class consisted of first through eighth grades. The Laws Schoolhouse was located a short ¼ mile north of Laws on the west side of Joe Smith Road. The author has names of some of the students.

matter how terrible a thing we did. Once when Hugh (my brother) and I were little, Pa came out and found a window broken in his truck. He suspected my brother Hugh as the culprit. He confronted Hugh and said it looked like the window in the old gray truck had been broken by a hammer or a rock. Hugh said, "I think it was a rock." That was the end of the conversation. Another time, Hugh and I took a red surveyor's crayon and drew large ambulance crosses (who knows why) all over Pa's pickup. There were huge crosses on the doors and panels. Pa drove around for months with all that mess on his truck and never said a word to either of us. He was meant to be with kids. Among Pa's other students (besides Hugh and me) were future well-known individuals including Horace Albright, second director of the National Park Service, and Curly

23

Fletcher, writer and poet (author of the song *Strawberry Roan*).

During his early years in Owens Valley, Pa and his father also provided music for dances around the Valley. Pa played a fiddle (which I still have) that he purchased from Clay Hampton, a teacher in Owens Valley in the nineteenth century. Mr. Hampton was one of Pa's elementary school teachers.

Pa married Angie McGovern in 1915, but later divorced (Pa had two children with Angie, Hugh Enloe and Arlene Mabel). On December 2, 1931, he married my grandmother, Edith Levy (she had been one of his students) and they had one child, my mother, Arlene. The Levys are another pioneer family from Independence. No kinder grandmother existed than my grandmother, E-ah, another one of my brother Hugh's original names. She was known as Edie to her friends. My grandfather had five grandchildren, Jim Brierly, Judith

Downtown Independence, California, in the early 1900s.
The picture is of the Independence Hotel owned by the author's grandmother's family, the Levys.

Left to right, A. A. Brierly (in his surveying outfit—high-topped lace-up boots, with pants tucked in), the author's mother Arlene, and the author's grandmother Edith. Taken in Independence, California in 1938.

Brierly (son and daughter of Hugh Brierly), Hugh Pearce, Mark Pearce, and me (sons of Arlene). My cousin Jim and his family live in Japan, my brother Mark and his wife live in Morro Bay, California, and I live in Bishop, California. Judith died of polio in 1954, and my brother Hugh died in 1989 while piloting a Delaware National Guard helicopter.

My grandfather endured many personal hardships. His daughter Arlene Mabel Brierly died at birth on June 12, 1916, and his son Hugh Brierly, a graduate of UCLA Law School, who went on to become Superior Court Judge of Inyo County (at that time the youngest man in the State holding that position) died at age thirty-six.

After his teaching career, my grandfather had many other Inyo County jobs including Undersheriff (1913-1915), Special Deputy (1915-1982), Superintendent of Schools (1922-1926), Probation Officer (1927), Tax Assessor (1928-1934), and Surveyor (1934-1970). His career as Surveyor alone was impressive. He was a licensed land and mineral surveyor in California and Nevada. He taught himself calculus and many other aspects of the surveyor's trade. Thanks to my grandfather, somewhere in the Inyo County Recorder's office are two special maps. He let my older brother and me each draw a complete map (with his help) of one of his surveys; in the bottom corner are the initials HP or RP, for my brother or me.

During his tenure as Undersheriff he became acquainted with a criminal named Cliff Ragan. His tales about Cliff Ragan were some of my favorites. When Cliff was in jail for one of his numerous crimes, Pa told me he used to talk with him. When Cliff was sentenced to San Quentin, my grandfather purchased his saddle and silver-mounted bit, which we still have. Cliff must have been quite a character. Pa said Cliff had been in San Quentin three times, Nevada State Penitentiary twice, and Idaho State Penitentiary once. Cliff's crimes included everything from horse stealing to seed theft. Cliff told him that being in prison was a "poor man's paradise." Cliff said he would behave well, get to be a trustee, and receive privileges to go outside and hunt for the other inmates. Besides, he was fed and had a place to sleep. He told Pa of being chased by a posse and having them fire their weapons at him and how exciting it was to hear the bullets whiz by.

Pa was a life-long livestock rancher in the Valley. He was given a heifer calf when he was two years old and his wish was to live to be 102 so he could have been in the cattle business for one hundred years. He missed that by only four years, living ninety-eight. The cattle brand he used was first registered in Tulare County, California, in 1858 by Hugh Enloe, his grandfather. During his life, Pa raised registered Morgan horses, Belgian draft horses, Corriedale sheep, shorthorn cattle, cross-bred cattle, and commercial pigs. Pa's ranch was one of the last places in the Owens Valley to use draft horses for farming. Pa continued to use his big Belgian draft horses into the 1960s. The horses were used primarily to put up meadow hay to feed to cattle. He worked draft horses a good portion of his life. He told of cleaning the big irrigation canals with teams of horses when he was a young man. When I was in high school, he took me to the ranch and laid out all the harness, driving lines, fifth chains, double trees, stretchers, and all the assorted equipment needed to put together a six-up horse hitch. He showed me how it all went together. We were only missing the horses. I wish I could have been a part of that era of the family ranch.

Pa was interested in a host of topics, including mineralogy, history, astronomy, geology, engineering, and Native American history, to name just a few. Pa was well read and knowledgeable in many subjects. Early in life, he took correspondence courses in mineralogy, blowpipe analysis for

From left to right, the author's older brother Hugh, A. A. Brierly, and the author, taken in Fort Lewis, Washington, 1962. Pa was telling one of his stories that we always enjoyed.

mineral identification, and civil engineering. His desire to learn and to educate himself was amazing. His retention of information was phenomenal.

During his life, he was actively involved in multiple community affairs and was a member of many national and local organizations including the following: Selective Service Board (twenty years), Inyo County Planning Commission, Inyo County Democratic Central Committee, Inyo-Mono Counties Coordinating Council, Independence Lions Club, Independence Civic Club, Owens Valley Unified School Board, and the Oddfellows Lodge.

His historical interests are shown by his memberships in the Cole County (Missouri) Historical Society, Cass County (Missouri) Historical Society, Missouri Historical Society, Eastern Sierra Historical Society, and the California Historical Society.

My grandfather's devotion to agriculture was illustrated by his memberships in the National Cattlemen's Association, California Cattlemen's Association, Inyo County Cattlemen's Association (he was a founder and the author of the bylaws), Morgan Horse Association, Belgian Horse Association, California Wool Growers Association, and the California Farm Bureau. Furthermore, he was a state director for the California Cattlemen's Association for a number of years.

He was also one of the original members of Bakersfield Production Credit Association. He was a life member of the American Congress on Surveying and Mapping and, for over forty years, a member of the American Institute of Mining and Metallurgical Engineers.

Pa received several awards in his life. He was featured in *Who's Who on the Pacific Coast* in 1951. The

Daughters of the American Revolution awarded him their Honor Medal award in 1977. The "Father of the Year" award was presented to Pa in 1970 by the Inyo-Mono Cowbelles.

After Pa's retirement from the County, he continued to operate his ranch until just before his death. Some of my fondest memories are hearing Pa honk his horn when he arrived at the ranch on weekends. I would be working on my FFA steer projects and he would drive in, give a toot, and we would sit and talk at length.

During his later years, he was sought after by historians of all types. Many individuals, from locals in-

From left to right, Edith Brierly (author's grandmother) Hugh Pearce (author's older brother), A. A. Brierly (author's grandfather), Mark Pearce (author's younger brother), and the author. Taken in Bishop, California, 1971. The two dogs are JJ and Sadie.

terested in Owens Valley history to University faculty and students, sought out his knowledge about the Owens Valley. He was interviewed by the *National Geographic* staff and quoted in their magazine. Ralph Story Television produced a segment on the Owens Valley, and the show contained an interview with Pa. Dr. Robert Levinson, a professor at San Jose State University, interviewed him about Jewish history in the Owens Valley. Charles Delameter interviewed him as part of his Masters thesis at California State University, Fullerton. Pa also wrote many historical articles for the *Inyo Register*, as well as being the focus of many articles by other *Register* writers. He also wrote for the Eastern California Museum newsletter.

One of his biggest pleasures in life was genealogy. He spent a good portion of his "retirement" years tracing his family tree. Much of what he learned he compiled for all of us to enjoy.

My grandfather, Arlie Brierly, lived a remarkable life and achieved a professional competency that few can claim. His legacy has influenced me in many ways. I learned to love seeking knowledge and, in general, to love a rural livestyle. He touched the lives of many people. Considering that his formal learning consisted of a high school education and no more, his accomplishments are even more admirable. He was respected by many.

> Arlie's qualifications of leadership were best exemplified by the fact that he headed many departments of Inyo County government. He also exerted a strong moral leadership in the courthouse. If I ever had any doubts in performing my duties as District Attorney about the rightness or wrongness of a proposed ac-

tion in a given situation, I could always rely on Arlie for fine mature advice.

If you want to know what it was like way back, and if you want to get a feeling of the devotion of the pioneer citizen, all you have to do is talk to Arlie, and you can hear first-hand stories and also see a living example.

There is probably no single citizen of Inyo County who has offered more service to the Eastern Sierra. He is probably the most beloved man in Inyo County.

> — *Frank Fowles,*
> *Inyo County District Attorney,*
> *July 20, 1975*

It can be said of Arlie Brierly that his word is bond.

I consider his example as a citizen and public officer an outstanding code of ethics in the areas of leadership, trustworthiness, patriotism, and public service.

Mr. Brierly is a gifted speaker, thoroughly acquainted with national, state, and local history, and looks to the future with fervent belief in the Constitution of the United States of America and in our public institutions.

> — *Melvin Bernasconi,*
> *Superintendent of Schools,*
> *July 8, 1977*

He stressed the classics in literature. I still remember many poems he had us memorize. He was kind and just in every way.

— Kathryn Young, retired teacher and former pupil, 1977

He was a grand person and I enjoyed our time together. He had so much information to share.

— Charles Ellis Delameter, February 5, 1997

His service and devotion to Inyo County will not likely be replicated.

This biography is presented to illustrate the character of A. A. Brierly, "Pa," and show his knowledge about the Owens Valley. His description, as he told me, of the events in and around the sale of Owens Valley lands to DWP follows.

The Owens Valley and DWP Land Purchases

The following is presented as written in 1974.

I have been given this information by my eighty-nine-year-old grandfather, A. A. Brierly, and by W. A. (Gus) Cashbaugh, both living in Owens Valley at the time Los Angeles began the land purchases. Gus and my grandfather were deeply involved in the affairs of the Valley. Both my grandfather and Mr. Cashbaugh still live here and have been continuous residents of Inyo County, always active and concerned with the events of this valley.

Perhaps it is easier to make a villain out of a large city (Los Angeles Department of Water and Power, i.e., DWP) than to put the blame on other factors. In any event, the story, as it has been represented, has been readily accepted by all.

To begin, I shall give an idea of how the irrigation situation existed before the city of Los Angeles appeared on the scene.

The first irrigation in Owens Valley was done from the more accessible tributaries of the River, in and around Lone Pine, George's Creek (Manzanar), Independence, Aberdeen, Fish Springs, Big Pine, Bishop, and Round Valley, while water from the Owens River, itself, flowed south to Owens Lake, an alkali lake some twenty miles long and eight to ten miles wide.

As the Valley settled up, water from the Owens River was diverted by means of big ditches or canals to serve the farmers' needs. From the south, the ditches were as follows: the Stevens Ditch and the East Side Canal (the latter intended to irrigate the land east of the River and south of Independence and the only ditch diverted by a company of outside people).

The next canal north was the Sanger Ditch which irrigated lands east of the River, south and east of Big Pine. A Mr. Sanger built this ditch to irrigate land owned by him. He raised alfalfa and horses.

The next canal north was the Owens River and Big Pine Canal. It was built by a group of Big Pine farmers to irrigate land west of the River and in the vicinity of Big Pine. Its point of diversion was just north of the Collins Road (halfway between Bishop and Big Pine). A ditch not too far north of the Big Pine Ditch was built by a man by the name of Muller, but it soon went out of business.

Then there was the Dell Ditch and the Rawson Ditch built by groups of farmers on the west side of the River, while on the east side of the River were the A. O. Collins Ditch and the George Collins Ditch, both built by the men whose names they bore.

Farther north, and on the west side of the River, was the Farmers' Ditch built by a group of farmers using lands in that area.

Still farther north were the two ditches that were first in time, and first in use: the McNally Ditch and the Bishop Creek Ditch. The name Bishop Creek had nothing to do with the fact that this ditch caught the surplus water of Bishop Creek Ditch, but was so named because at that time (the late 1870s), the town of Bishop was known as Bishop Creek. The McNally Ditch and the Bishop Creek Ditch were both built by groups of farmers.

Last in time, but highest in point of diversion from the River, was the Owens River Canal, which was used to irrigate land south and west of Bishop. It, too, was constructed by a group of farmers in that area.

A diversion highest on a stream has great advantages, because if there is water in a stream, the highest diversion can take it. This is not a legal point, but a fact that only a lawsuit, or a shotgun, can stop.

There was no storage for water anyplace on the River, and the winter runoff continued to flow into a shrinking Owens Lake. About this time, the Reclamation Service began looking into the water situation, and around 1905 began surveys and other work necessary to plan for less wasteful use of water from the Owens River.

In the meantime, representatives of ditches from Big Pine, north, got together and formed an organization called Associated Ditches. They sent three men to Washington, D.C., to learn more about the plans of the Reclamation Service. While there, they learned that the policy of President Theodore Roosevelt was the guideline "The greatest good to the greatest number." This guideline was to apply to the use of Owens River water.

Meanwhile, the dry years continued and it became evident that Los Angeles was going to need more water for its expanding city (as it still does today).

Representatives from Associated Ditches met with representatives from Los Angeles, and a plan developed — the only plan that would have preserved Owens Valley as it was then.

This plan was to build a 100-foot dam (on what is now Crowley Lake), which would guarantee water to irrigate 30,000 acres — more acres than were then being irrigated.

At one of these meetings of Associated Ditches, W. A. Cashbaugh, president of Bishop Creek Ditch, was present as the elected representative because George Watterson was out of town. At this meeting, Ed Leahy, the Los Angeles representative, offered a plan whereby the City would drill nineteen deep wells and put electric pumps on them to pump the water. But the pumping plan and the foot dam were opposed by the Watterson brothers and by Fred Eaton, who had extensive holdings in Long Valley. Mr. Eaton was not just an ordinary local farmer for two reasons: first, he was a very large landowner. Second, he was a former mayor of Los Angeles.

Mr. Eaton and the Watterson brothers insisted on a 150-foot dam, regardless of the fact that engineering studies showed that the formations at the dam site would not support a dam that high. A dam that was 100-feet high would not flood the lands of Mr. Eaton, and, therefore, the City would not be forced to buy these lands from him.

About this time, Mr. Eaton and the Watterson brothers figured that an Irrigation District would stop the City. The dry years were continuing and Los Angeles had to have more water. Mr. Eaton was heard to remark "We've got them over a barrel" (meaning Los Angeles).

If the City's point of diversion had been above the proposed Irrigation District, it might have worked; but, as it was, the point of diversion was below the proposed Irrigation District, and all the City had to do was buy the land and not irrigate it. The water would then simply flow back into the River and the City would pick it up.

At the first public meeting, held in the Sunland school house, it was proposed that the Irrigation District include West Bishop and all the land irrigated from the River, but to leave the town of Bishop out. However, when the matter came to a vote, West Bishop was left out and the town of Bishop was included.

In the opinion of my grandfather, this is what changed Owens Valley. The town of Bishop, with no water to give to the Irrigation District, had more votes and was able to control all matters relating to the water situation.

Now, we begin to get into the real troubles by which many people were later hurt.

In many accounts written by local people years ago, there were still strong loyalties to old friendships, and so, sometimes, no blame was given to some who deserved it, because the writer did not want to hurt individuals or their families. That is one reason why many facts concerning the purchase of land and water rights by the city of Los Angeles were lost.

The other main issue contributing to the omission of many facts was that so many people were heavily in debt to the Wattersons' Inyo County Bank.

The proposed Irrigation District had to own the water and have an engineer, an attorney, an assessor, etc., all costing money. So, the next thing in order was a bond issue. A bond election was held and with the votes from the city of Bishop, a $425,000 bond issue passed.

It was not known at the time that the Inyo County Bank was in trouble, and this would not be known for sure until 1927 when the Bank went broke. In any event, at the time of the bond election, the Wattersons were all for it, because they needed that money in their bank to stabilize some of its problems. The Watterson brothers had a "finger in many pies," and it is interesting to note here that the bank president was also president of the Irrigation District.

When the Bank did fail, the Watterson brothers were in trouble for a number of things, but they were not asked about the $425,000. No one ever did know what happened to it.

During this time, a group of farmers (those not in favor of the bond issue) went to Sacramento to try to stop the sale of the bonds and were assured by the attorney general that the bonds would not be sold. After the farmers left, however, W. W. Watterson talked to the attorney general and, apparently, was able to convince him that all was in order and that the sale of bonds would be beneficial to all. The attorney general changed his mind.

So, as my grandfather says, "There we were, going into debt to buy something that *already belonged to us*, and to turn the management of it all over to the Inyo County Bank and the town of Bishop!"

The dry years continued and 30,000 inches of water were claimed by the ditches, while only 7,000 inches of water were in the River. Again, the local people already had problems, *not* caused by the city of Los Angeles.

The Owens River Canal people, being the highest on the River, and being perfectly willing to defend their position, had armed men at their intake to see that no one got any of the supply that they intended to take.

My grandfather also tells of some people (*local* people), higher up on the ditch that irrigated his ranch, not letting him have enough water. But a good friend, also higher up on the ditch, would turn the water down at night. My grandfather would irrigate at night, and in the morning, his friend would shut it off.

My grandfather feels strongly that if Los Angeles had not continued buying land, in spite of the Irrigation District, there would surely have been disastrous trouble between the farmers themselves.

It is good to remember, here, that in *many* accounts of history, not just in the Owens Valley, water has been the source of much trouble—killings, hard feelings, the list is endless. Water is considered sacred to the farmer or rancher whose livelihood depends upon it.

Denied the means to keep the Valley much as it was, by use of the proposed 100-foot dam and the proposed pumping, and running short of water, the City had to buy land; and buy, they did.

The McNally Ditch area was the first to sell. Good prices were paid and no one was compelled to sell. If a farmer or rancher didn't sell, he still received water. No one was frozen out.

Meanwhile, the president of the Inyo County Bank was making efforts to sell the whole Valley; he, of course, was to handle the details himself. However, by this time, a good number of local people had lost confidence in him and preferred to handle their own affairs.

Although this fact was not yet public knowledge, the Inyo County Bank was in financial trouble. The

Watterson brothers were in a desperate situation. They needed the money from the land sales to put into their bank.

The Big Pine people were the next to sell—at very good prices. Again, no one had to sell; they wanted to sell. And if a man did not sell, he still was furnished with whatever water he needed.

It might be a good time, right here, to make another point that is often overlooked. Many, many of these local farmers were barely making a living. They had small places and were just getting by. From other information that has since been published about these times, the whole Valley is described as a somewhat idyllic setting, with everything sounding as though it were being viewed through rose-colored glasses.

Bit by bit the selling-out to Los Angeles continued. A group under the Bishop Creek Ditch was the next. My grandfather was one of them—one of the negotiators for the sale, in fact. Therefore, he knows the prices paid and has always felt that, *for the times*, the prices were more than fair. My grandfather gives two examples of this. He knew one man who had tried to sell his land the previous year for $14,000, but who received $27,000 the following year when the City bought his place. Others thanked the negotiators of the sale for the prices they received.

Another man, Orrie Dunn, sold to the City but did not get his check when he thought he would and made some inquiries. The check had been sent to the Inyo County Bank and someone there had forged his name and cashed the check. This also happened to another couple my grandfather knew.

So, what changed the Owens Valley was not just the purchase of land and water by the city of Los Angeles, but also the Irrigation District, backed by power-hungry and financially pressed *local* people.

Another point, which must not be overlooked, is that one of the local newspapers, *The Owens Valley Herald*, owned by Harry Glasscock, was heavily in debt to the Inyo County Bank, which belonged to the Watterson brothers. This, in large part, accounts for another reason that so much of what has been written concerning the land sales in the Owens Valley was a very biased version.

Money has great power, and if a person is in debt to someone else (a bank or an individual), that person is not in a very good position to do much criticizing. Also, one other fact that is never stressed is that many, many of the local farmers were also in debt to the Inyo County Bank. Many would have lost their land because they were unable to pay off their mortgages. So the City's purchase of their little farms gave them the opportunity to pay off their debts and still have money left over.

Unfortunately, for many of them, they placed the money from their sales in the Inyo County Bank. So, when the Bank failed, they lost all their money. And that, in no way, was the fault of the city of Los Angeles.

The group called the Associated Ditches was formed to handle water matters for their area. This group, consisting of one man from each of the large canals, discussed the water affairs with the city of Los Angeles. William Symons represented the McNally Ditches; George Watterson (uncle of Mark and Wilfred Watterson), who was secretary of the Bishop Creek Canal, represented the people of the Bishop Creek Canal area; Charlie Partridge represented the Owens River

Canal; Will Hines represented the Big Pine Ditch; and Went Ford represented the Ford-Rawson Ditch.

In most of the stories about the water situation in the Owens Valley, three men are described as "traitors." These men were Lester C. Hall, an attorney, William Symons, and George Watterson.

This is one point in my information from Mr. Cashbaugh, that he strongly stresses is so unfair. These were prominent local people who had been here for a long time, and whose love and concern for the welfare of the Valley was as great as anyones!

When the farmers began selling to Los Angeles, Mr. Hall was the attorney handling most of these matters.

Emotions were very high during these times. My grandfather and Mr. Cashbaugh tell this story about what happened to Mr. Hall.

> One evening, while Mr. Hall was eating at a restaurant, a truck driver came in and dragged him outside. There, he was taken by several men in Klu Klux Klan clothing and handcuffed. Then they threatened his life. He became frightened by the group, and because he was a Mason, he gave the Mason sign for "distress." It must have reached the conscience of some Mason who was in the group, for one of the men released him. He made his way from near Rossi Hill to the George Warren residence, a little north of Big Pine, where he found safety. Mr. Warren was a friend and another one of the people against the formation of the Irrigation District.

Mr. Warren was a director of the Irrigation District, but had been involved in helping to sell the Big Pine Ditch. He was threatened to such an extent that he kept a revolver buckled on him wherever he went and had farmer friends guarding his place.

George Watterson (one of those unjustly branded as a traitor) was ordered out of town. Later, after the Wattersons' Inyo County Bank failed and hurt so many people, Mr. Watterson told my grandfather that he was ashamed to have the name of Watterson.

Will Symons, who sold at the time of the McNally Ditch, had helped negotiate the settlement with the City, along with George Watterson, that would have made it possible to keep the Valley as it had been. Symons felt that he was in such jeopardy that he never came to town without a loaded shotgun on the seat beside him. Watterson and Symons were branded as traitors by the local press.

Mr. Cashbaugh tells how he and my grandfather and their friends were harassed by the community. They were called "those skunks on the Bishop Creek Canal," and men in cars would drive by their homes with masks over their faces.

The Irrigation District brought in an attorney, Mr. Boone. He must have been a very decent sort for, although he represented the group opposing my grandfather and the above-mentioned men, he took the following action. One day he stopped my grandfather in the street, took him into the entrance of the stairs in a building, and said he saw how things were going here. He said to my grandfather, "You, Gus Cashbaugh, and Tom Williams, be careful," for the Watterson brothers and their followers didn't want to lose control of things, and were taking every means to prevent it.

With the other ditches selling out, the Owens River Canal people who wanted to sell became worried. If they had not wanted to sell, they did not need to sell. They were the highest on the river and could take all the water they wanted, regardless of what took place below them. But they wanted to sell and show the City that it had better buy their land, too. The radicals among them joined with a large number of local businessmen and seized the spillway on the aqueduct north of Lone Pine (Alabama Gates).

Businessmen in Bishop at that time were frightened that the town would no longer have any business and that the Valley was going to dry up and blow away. They had good reason to be concerned. Those were times of great change and much stress. They were stepping into an unknown future. Change is difficult at any time, but the radical change that the Owens Valley was undergoing during those years certainly put human nature to a number of hard tests. However, this is a slightly different version than what has been publicized about the seizure of the spillway by the farmers who were trying to keep the City from taking Owens River water!

My grandfather was in Bishop the day the spillway was seized and most of the businesses were closed. Not all of the businessmen took part in this affair. Tom Williams left town permanently that day. He, in no way, wanted any part of the radicals and their plans for seizing the spillway. In any event, these radicals had resorted to dynamite, intimidation, and violence to gain their ends.

The Watterson brothers were *not* bad men. They had done many favors for local people. They had loaned money to keep some of these ranchers and farmers going. They had done kind, personal favors for people. To this day, Mr. Cashbaugh does not want to say anything really bad against them. They had all grown up together and had been friends, as well as being on opposing sides in this city of Los Angeles affair. My grandfather feels the same way. In spite of all that took place, some of these loyalties are unbelievably strong. To understand the predicament that the Wattersons were in which caused them to take such desperate measures is admirable.

My grandfather also tells of some action proposed by some of the more radical followers of the Wattersons. They planned to meet my grandfather and some others on the road after one of their trips to Los Angeles to negotiate their sales and warn them not to come back to Owens Valley. But, Mr. Watterson, the bank president, heard of it and stopped them. So, apparently, he still felt the pull of old loyalties and friendships, too.

Dynamite was used, not only on wells, but some was set out in a field near my grandfather's home—to scare him, I suppose. My grandfather carried a pistol all the time and slept with a loaded shotgun by his bedside. Another man, Joe Garner, slept in an empty silo with a shotgun by his side also.

The times were hectic and troubled. Later, Mr. Garner became so distraught by all this that he committed suicide. To quote my grandfather, "He was a victim of those farmers who *now* are credited with fighting the City's purchase of the land in the Owens Valley when, in fact, they were doing everything they could to force the City to buy *their* land."

I want to make it extremely clear that in no way am I labeling the Watterson brothers as bad men. They were not bad, only human beings who had overextended themselves financially and were caught in a desperate situation that caused them to try some extreme measures to cover their mistakes. At all times, my grandfather feels, the Wattersons thought they could make good on their dealings and get the money back in the bank. It never was their intent to hurt people as they did. In the end, they were sent to San Quentin paying a very high price for their mistakes.

When it came to the final purchase of the Owens River Canal lands, the city of Los Angeles and the radicals in this group agreed to an Appraisal Committee, composed of George Naylor, Chairman of the Inyo County Board of Supervisors; Viv Jones, Inyo County Assessor; and Grant Clark, Inyo County Treasurer, a man of countrywide knowledge and experience.

These men appraised every parcel of land that was sold, and the only criticism my grandfather ever heard was when some farmer said, "My neighbor got more than I did." Not one of them ever felt he got less than his property was worth.

The Barlow Ranch* is a good example of one of the old ranches that didn't sell. They have always had water and sold their property only recently to be subdivided by a private individual. The Chance Ranch, the Evans and Arcularius Ranches in Round Valley had

---

* Other examples of ranches not purchased by DWP but later sold and subdivided are: Matlick Ranch, McLaren Ranch (McLaren Tract), Reynolds Ranch (Rolling Green Terrace), Rasin Ranch (West Ridge Manor), forty acres (Round Valley), Wilkerson Ranch (Wilkerson Tract), and Lazy A. This is an important point to note. Many lands not sold to DWP and not kept in agriculture ended up as subdivisions and mobile home parks. Again, this illustrates that land ownership by DWP in the Owens Valley keeps the land open for public use.

been private land until very recently. Part of the Arcularius Ranch is still in private ownership. The Cashbaughs still own private land in Long Valley. The old Schabbell Ranch near Independence remained in private ownership until the death of the last of the Schabbell brothers. And the Spainhower Ranch in Lone Pine is still privately owned.

There are others who did not sell to Los Angeles in the early 1900s and apparently operated very well without any difficulties with the City, contrary to the stories about how the City "forced" people out.

Those were fearful days, and the entire truth has never been told. The town of Bishop was worried, and justly so, as I mentioned earlier. Bishop was where the newspapers were located, and the news they put out was awfully biased.

George Watterson and Will Symons were two of the men who negotiated a settlement that might have kept the Valley as it was. Instead of being honored for their actions, both men were branded as traitors by the local press.

The troubles with the city of Los Angeles do not compare to the trouble among the local people at that time. Most of the farmers were in debt to the Inyo County Bank, and did not dare to oppose anything the bank wanted. The bank, itself, through injudicious investments, was in a terrible mess; a mess that had been coming on for some time. "So we all found out later," says my grandfather, who found this out himself when he received his last payment of $18,000 on the land he had sold to the City. He received the check and deposited it in the bank on July 28, 1927, and the bank failed on August 4, 1927.

A bank receiver was sent to take over, and my grandfather asked him how far in the hole the bank was. The reply was, "Somewhere between three and a half and five million dollars."

Again, my grandfather points out that the Watterson brothers had their hands in everything. The Natural Soda Products Company never did pay, but the Wattersons were paying dividends on that stock out of bank funds. Watterson Brothers, Inc. had large holdings under the Bishop Creek Ditch, which sold for $300,000. The stockholders never received a cent. Another friend of my grandfather's, Jean Blanc, received dividends from stock he was supposed to own in the Bank, but when the Bank failed, the stock had been disposed of, even though he was still getting dividends from stocks that no longer existed.

A whole book could be written about the Watterson brothers and their financial dealings. It was very extensive, and quite confusing to me. In any event, they served time in San Quentin when their world finally came crashing down around them, and, unfortunately, upon the many people who had money in their bank.

Again, the loyalties of those people for one another is astounding. My great-grandmother, Rachel Brierly, was a character witness for the Wattersons during their trial. She, like my grandfather and many others, never felt the Wattersons ever intended that their actions would harm anyone. That they did is one more sad event in those troubled times.

The entire topic of the land purchases by the city of Los Angeles in the Owens Valley is a very complex one. One of the most tragic aspects of the entire matter is that such biased stories have been published. Mr.

Chalfant's *Story of Inyo* is an excellent book, but I feel its biggest failure is that in it he tried to cover far too many topics. His omission of both sides of the story about the City and the land purchases was unfortunate. Mr. Chalfant's book is used almost as a "bible" of facts about Inyo County. Because it is used as a reference so much by later writers, the one-sided presentation of the City's dealings with the farmers has continued.

It is my hope that this brief report, based on the stories given to me by people who were actually involved with the city of Los Angeles during the time of the land purchases, will at least give someone an insight into the other side of this much-written-about story.

The above description about DWP (the City) and the Owens Valley, as mentioned, was written in 1974 for my senior civics class. This version of the information on land purchases by DWP is authentic in that it is written from a compilation of the recollections of two prominent Valley residents, my grandfather A.A. Brierly and Gus Cashbaugh.

The Controversy in Brierly's Own Words

The following is a transcript from an interview conducted by Charles Ellis Delameter (Delameter, 1977) as part of the research for his Masters Thesis at California State University Fullerton. The interview was conducted on November 19, 1976, when my grandfather was ninety-two years old. Mr. Delameter interviewed several individuals in the Owens Valley in regard to their views about the Los Angeles Department of Water and Power's land purchases. I present this as a followup to the previous chapter. This interview is important in that it is in my grandfather's own words. Some of the material is repeated in this chapter and the previous, but there is also a wealth of new information contained in the interview.

Interviewee:	A. Brierly (**B**)
Interviewer:	E. Delameter (**D**)
Subject:	O.V. Controversy

D: This is an interview with Mr. Arlie A. Brierly for the California State University at Fullerton, Environmental Studies Program by Ellis Delameter. This interview is being conducted at approximately 10:00 a.m. at Mr. Brierly's residence at 454 N. Edwards, Independence, California on November 19, 1976.

D: Mr. Brierly, I would like to start the interview today by asking you to talk a little bit about where you were born and where you were raised.

B: I was born a half mile south of the town of Bishop on the east side of the highway. There is a building there now, but it isn't the building I was born in. I was raised here in the Valley. My folks came to Inyo County and landed in Bishop the 2nd of May, 1876. There have been some of us here ever since.

D: What year were you born?

B: 1884.

D: What do you recall of your days here in the Valley?

B: Well, that is kind of hard to answer.

D: What was it like here?

B: Well, I can tell you one thing...when I finished grammar school there was no high school here in the Valley, so my folks sent me to Los Angeles. Of course, we went there and stayed the year around because there was no automobile travel and no trains. You could come to Mojave on the train and then take a horse stage to Keeler. Then, you would take the narrow gauge railroad on to Bishop, or, come with your own outfit.

Two different times I left Los Angeles in June and landed in Bishop on the 2nd of July. It was eleven days on the road from Los Angeles to Bishop, so this was kind of a little country all by itself. There was a lot of trading going on. People didn't have much money. That old clock up there, I remember when we got it. The clock we had before that got acid in it and ate the spring out. Anyway, we needed a new one.

There was a jeweler in Bishop, and his name was R. W. Scott. He lived on a homestead east of Bishop and drove back and forth everyday if he needed horse feed in town. My mother was a trader and went to see if she could trade hay for the clock. Well, he didn't need any hay right then, but traded the clock anyway. When he wanted hay, the folks didn't have any. But, the next door neighbor did. My grandfather had dried peaches, so they traded dried peaches to the fellow who had the hay, to get the clock.

D: What did you do when you finished your school years?

B: I came here [to Independence]. In those days the County Board of Education gave you the teacher's examination. I took the teacher's examination and got a certificate to teach school, and commenced teaching here in Independence, the 2nd of September, 1905. I haven't lived here always, however. Independence has been my home for the last forty years. Before that I lived in Bishop. My mother was the first woman in Inyo County to file a homestead on government land. She later lost it, but I don't know why. We [meaning the family, my grandfather A.A. Brierly wasn't born yet] were living on it, but later had to get off. I think there was trouble because she wasn't married; wasn't the head of a family, and had no right to file a homestead. That was about the size of it and I think, probably that was what threw the thing out. She was the only one in her family that accumulated any property.

My father told me though, that he never realized that all this open, vacant land would be located sometime. He never thought about it, but she did. At one time she had 320 acres within 2 miles of the town of Bishop.

D: What did she grow on the land?

B: Well, in the first place it didn't grow much. They just lived on it to get title to it. They raised alfalfa and wheat and corn, one thing and another. My grandfather was a horticulturist. He had a ten-acre orchard in Bishop. It was the largest one in the country at that time. He was 59 when he came to Bishop. My mother had 80 acres that he worked after that and he planted an orchard, cleared 40 or 50 acres of sagebrush, and he planted it in alfalfa. In those days he would be a senior citizen and supposed to quit. Those old-timers didn't quit until they had to.

D: I guess agriculture was really booming in the early days.

B: The farmers barely made a living. The thing that finally put the farmers on their feet here in the Valley was the discovery of gold at Tonopah. Then, there was a markup for their hay and everything they had.

D: What year was that?

B: Well, I can't tell you exactly. It was after 1905, anyway. The only people who ever made money here years ago were the sheep men. Of course, they summered their sheep here and then they drove them over to Bakersfield and put them on the grass there for the winter. They drove them back here the next spring. There was a man out here who could tell you about the sheep business. Some herders took a bunch of sheep up to Mammoth for the summer. They didn't take them to

Mammoth, they took them to the Goldfield and sold them. They got caught though, and sent up for it.

I've got an article about the first cattle that came here to the Valley in 1859. They were brought here by an uncle of mine, by marriage. That was the time when the Mono Diggins were boomin'. The cattle provided something to eat and protection from the Indians. There was a bunch of gamblers and a woman who said she was the daughter of Kit Carson. When they got here to Lone Pine, they met a man from the Mono Diggins who told Ketchum, [my uncle] they [the Mono Diggins] weren't what they were cracked up to be. Ketchum stopped the cattle here but went on up and the woman who said she was the daughter of Kit Carson went to Mono Lake, too. My uncle had a younger uncle with him, and the only trouble they had was when one of the men got into a row over this woman. I think at Mono Lake there was quite a [newspaper] article about Kit Carson's daughter, telling what kind of woman she was. You can imagine what kind of woman she was, coming in with a bunch of cowboys and gamblers who were going to Mono Diggins.

D: Do you remember the talk that first hit the Valley about Los Angeles taking water down to the City?

B: That was about 1905. There was a hullabaloo here and a lot of gossip got going that dust would be blowing in the streets of Independence. You can look out there now and see what it is like. A lot of things like that went on that caused bad feelings. I know when I came here to teach they were talking about it in the Valley.

D: You said the tempers got pretty high. Was there any violence or anything done that embroiled the people against the City?

B: Not by the farmers, no. The real trouble came on when the City bought up all these ranches and town had nothing to go on.* It was the townspeople that were violent. Of course, they had access and the power of publicity. Glasscock and Chalfant published that stuff and that kind of riled people up sometimes.

This L. C. Hall they came darn near lynching, was a lawyer for some people who had sold to the City. He didn't have any property. I think that he was at a lunch counter in Bishop when a husky fellow walked in behind him, threw his arms around his neck, pulled him off, and took him toward Rossi Hill and threatened him. I don't know what they were going to do to him, but he was a Mason and he made the Masonic distress sign. In the Masons when you make a distress sign somebody comes to your assistance [if they are a Mason]. I was in West Bishop the night that happened. The farm bureau was pretty good here then, and I was at a farm bureau meeting that evening when the news came about what they had done to Hall.

D: Can you tell me a little bit about the Associated Ditches?

B: Well, the members were the McNally Ditch, Bishop Creek Ditch, Owens River Canal, the Big Pine Ditch and the Rawson Ditch. I think there were five major ditches. The City wanted water and the farmers knew

---

* "Nothing to go on" means that the local community businesses depended on Owens Valley ranches and farms for business. When DWP bought the ranches and farms there was no agricultural base to support the town businesses.

they were going to get it, so they formed an organization that negotiated with the City. They had a settlement agreed on with [the City], which if they had been left alone, the City could get what water they wanted and that area around Bishop would still be irrigated. You know, you find these things out later. The farmers didn't know that the bank up there was in a fix. I found out later that Fred Eaton owed the bank a lot of money and the only way he could get the money was to have a 150-foot dam in Long Valley that would flood him. The City agreed to a 100-foot dam on it. He wanted the City to pay him for the 150-foot dam. The City [refused] and commenced buying land. So, the heads of the Associated Ditches, William Symons, George Watterson, George Warren, and I think Charles Partridge, good, respectable, honest farmers, went for it.

D: I've read that the Owens Valley Protective Association came along then. What brought that about?

B: Was that when they started that Irrigation District?

D: It was right before they started the district.

B: Well, I don't remember that right now.

D: I had read in one of the newspapers, *The Owens Valley Herald*, that the Owens Valley Protective Association was formed, I gather, because [the local people] were discontent with what the Associated Ditches were doing, or the lack of progress they were making with the City.

B: That's probably what it was, and probably why I didn't know anything about them. What the Associated Ditches was trying to do, if they had been left alone would have been fine, but the agreement that they had with the City was upset.

D: One particular newspaper that I read was very slanderous I would say, to some of the people of the Valley, mainly the directors of the Associated Ditches. Can you give me any idea why it was so bitter against these individuals?

B: Well, they blamed a lot of this Associated Ditches business on to George Watterson and Will Symons. Glasscock, the editor of *The Owens Valley Herald*, had no assets, owed the bank a lot of money, and was under their [the bank's] control. Of course as I say, we didn't realize the bank was up against it. When the bank failed and the receiver was here I asked him one time how much the bank was in the hole. He said between 3 1/2 and 5 million dollars. Where the hell it all went to, I don't know.

The people in Bishop voted in the Irrigation District and voted bonds. The farmers didn't do it, because they already owned the water. They were going into debt to buy something that already belonged to them and turn the management over to Bishop. That was where the sticker was.

D: I see. Is that why the directors of the Associated Ditches were so firm against the formation of the Irrigation District?

B: Yes. I was against it, too. In fact, I made a trip to Sacramento to see the Attorney General to see if I could get the sale of these bonds stopped. They sold for, I think, $425,000 and nobody ever asked where the money went. Wilfred Watterson was the head of the whole damned thing. He was the head of the bank and the Protective Association. Nobody ever asked him what they did with the money. Nobody knows what they did with it.

They [the Watterson brothers] had what they called the Natural Soda Products down here east of Keeler, that wasn't paying. They took money out of the bank to pay dividends on the stock for that place. That didn't get into the papers. I know a fellow, Orrie Dunn, who sold to the City. The money didn't come and didn't come. Finally, he went to the City and come to find out, the City had mailed the check to the bank. The bank had forged his name and cashed it.

There was another prominent man by the name of Charlie Summers. He was a cattle man and I heard they had forged his name; so I asked him. He said, "Yes, they forged my name and my wife's too." Those were red hot times. Lots of people packed a gun. George Warren wasn't the only one; he just had his out where you could see it. If someone ever tried to take him out of the country, somebody would have been hurt.

D: I've read that he was approached and told to get out of the country.

B: Oh, yeah, and he was not going. He had all those farmers of Big Pine behind him. George Watterson was an uncle to Wilford and Mark. He was ordered out of the town and as it happened he was getting ready to leave.

D: Mr. Brierly, you have handed me an article which you have written called, "Water in Owens Valley," and I would like to, with your permission, include this in our final transcript.

B: That's all right, as long as I get the original back.

D: In your article, you talked about being forced to carry a weapon. Would you like to elaborate on that a little bit?

B: Well, when we got around to selling Bishop Creek Ditch, a bunch of fellows, including Gus Cashbaugh and myself went down to Los Angeles to sell our land to the City. This radical bunch, I guess the Owens Valley Protective Association, heard about it and they called a meeting. They were going to meet us down the road and tell us not to come back. Watterson stopped that.

One time I went upstairs in the building on East Line and Main [in Bishop] to see a doctor. When I came out, here at the head of the stairs, was one of those radical bunches watching to see where I had gone. Two different times they set dynamite off within a quarter of a mile of the house. I couldn't imagine what was the matter and I asked somebody. He said they were trying to scare me. So, I got a pistol. Will Symons never came to town in the car without the curtains closed and a loaded shotgun on the seat beside him. They never got him either. They caught Hall when he wasn't looking.

D: The newspaper accounts seem to be very bitter against Hall, personally.

B: Oh, yeah, he was a lawyer for the farmers of the McNally Ditch when they were selling to the City. I knew Hall, knew him well. He was a very, very fine man. He was a good man. When they had him out there south of Bishop on the mountain they did get him to promise to leave here and never come back. He didn't, he never came back here.

D: You owned property on which ditch?

B: Bishop Creek Ditch.

D: How much property did you own, Mr. Brierly?

B: Seventy-five inches of water. Those ditches were put in by the farmers, too. No outside capital put them in. In fact, my uncle helped build that ditch. The Bishop Creek Ditch and the McNally Ditch were the two first in time, and the first in use. The Owens River Canal, I guess maybe we mentioned, was the first appropriating any water. Of course, that was the highest up on the river and any water that came along, they took it.

D: What prompted your ditch to decide to sell to the City?

B: The Irrigation District coming up. That's the thing that wrecked this country. The farmers going into debt to buy something that already belonged to them and turn the control over to the town of Bishop, where Bishop had the most votes.

D: I see, you feel that most of the trouble was caused by the townspeople rather than the farmers.

B: Sure, it was. The farmers had no kick a coming. They didn't have to sell unless they wanted to. That's another thing; some of them didn't sell. As long as they were on those ditches they got water. The City let them have water. I had charge of Bishop Creek Ditch for awhile up there, and that was the instructions. "Anybody who hadn't sold out, give them water." Some of them liked to drowned out everything because they had water, water, water.

D: One of the accounts claimed that a lot of the farmers were forced out because the City was "checkerboarding."

B: The only reason they were "checkerboarding", was because this fellow wanted to sell out and the next one didn't. They would buy anybody that wanted to sell out.

Of course, that area south of Bishop called Sunland was largely small tracts of ground. If they sold out they wouldn't get much, so they held out. Finally, a committee was appointed by the chairman of the board of supervisors. The county assessor and the county tax collector put a value on a piece of ground. I never heard anybody kick about the price they put on it, except one fellow who said that his land wasn't valued like somebody elses. When people get filled full of thoughts it's sometimes hard to shake them.

I was told, I don't know how true it is, that when the City came in to buying stuff in here, as far as the law was concerned they didn't have to pay any taxes at all. The assemblyman from here, George Clark, claimed that he changed the law, and Matthews, from Los Angeles, claimed he changed the law. So, it was fixed so that taxes had to be paid by everyone. If any improvements were made, they didn't have to pay taxes on them.

D: After the City would buy a piece of land, if the property was involved with a water ditch, would they maintain it?

B: The ditch was maintained. In fact, there were only two or three ranches left on the East Side Canal for years and years, but they always got water. The trouble was that the ditches high up were taking the water out.

D: I've read that there were a lot of orchards in the Valley in the early 20s.

B: Oh, yeah, in the area south of Bishop called Sunland. I think there were some orchards down here south of Independence near Manzanar. One trouble with the orchards was the early frost. [Prices were another problem.] They would have a big apple crop and the price was no good.

D: I read about the Pear Growers Association.

B: Yes, pears seem to miss that early frost, but I don't think there was ever very many of them.

D: I understand they were promoted mainly to increase the value of the land, to protect the land and the water rights.

B: That might be, yes. I was talking to W. B. Mathews, the city attorney when the City was buying up all the land. "Well," he said, "You were in the path of progress." That's it. So many people down here wanted more water and are still fussing about water.

D: You mentioned in your article that dynamiting was used to blow up some of the wells. Was that a regular occurrence back in those days?

B: Some of them were blowing them up just to be doing it. I remember on Collins Road, this side of Bishop, across the river was a well. Well, they blew that well up. There were so many things happening, you kind of forget.

D: In the one article that I read in *The Owens Valley Herald* written by Mr. Glasscock, he called these particular individuals you mentioned earlier, traitors. Apparently that stirred people up a lot.

B: Oh, sure it did. They all had access to publicity; the farmers didn't.

D: You mentioned that Glasscock was indebted to the Wattersons or to their bank. Do you feel that was his main motive for being so bitter against these individuals? He was supporting the Wattersons?

B: Yeah. In fact, he committed suicide right after the bank failed.

D: Oh, is that right?

B: Yeah. That bank that was dealing with the farm business should have been in first class shape because the farmers were getting money to pay off their indebtedness.

Nobody ever checked on them to see where all that money went. I know there was a fellow in Los Angeles, I think he was gambling in oil stocks. Some people thought that Wilford Watterson was tied in with him. I've forgotten his name.

D: I read about an attempted diversion that the City made around the Big Pine Ditch. Did you hear about that?

B: Yeah, in fact, I think I told the Big Pine Ditch [group] what was going on, because I happened to see it. George Warren was the one that I went and told what the City was doing.

D: What was his reaction?

B: Well, that's when they stopped it. One thing about George Warren, you didn't have to guess where he was. He was outspoken. He was a member of the board of directors of the Irrigation District, too, for awhile. He didn't do what Watterson said. Watterson was the head of the Irrigation District, too. In fact, he had a plaster* on every ranch in the country pretty near, and every farmer had to [go to them].

---

* Refers to Watterson holding a lot of "paper," i.e., bank notes, etc. on the local ranchers and farmers. The term comes from something "was plastered with paper."

I remember one man, in particular. We used to meet on the street corners and talk. Different boys said that he had sold out to the City. A day or two came along and he hadn't sold to the City. He talked different because the Wattersons had a plaster on him. The Wattersons were too free in making their loans, for one thing. I am sure that was the reason the people thought so much of them.

My mother was a character witness when the trial was going on here. One thing about them though, they never tried to lay the bad feelings on anybody else. They did it.

One thing happened after that was all over, I've always wondered about. I met Mark Watterson going east on Warm Spring Road. Well, I wondered what he was doing going east on that road. I couldn't turn around and follow him, but later I did follow his tracks and he went down to the river, crossed, and went quite a ways. I always wondered what the devil he was doing up there. Did he have some money hid up there, or what? The bank receiver, too, told me he was sure that the Wattersons themselves had access to a pot of money somewhere. I know one man who was a supporter of this racket whose wife bought an automobile and paid cash for it. She must have gotten some money somewhere. There is a sister of the Wattersons living out here two or three miles. She thinks they are all right. There was another sister, I went to school with. I said to her, "Wilford was the one that got the bank in trouble, and that if Mark had been handling it they wouldn't have come up short." She said, "Mark is no weakling."

D: I guess in 1924 there was a lot of dynamiting of the aqueduct.

B: I don't remember the year, but there was, down here, yeah.

D: Well, what do you think about that?

B: I think it was a piece of damned nonsense.

D: Do you?

B: Yeah. They said they were trying to stop the City from buying. That wasn't it at all. They were trying to force the City to buy.

You know, after a lot of negotiating in the town, they got reparations. I think four times the assessed valuation. For instance, on this lot you could sell all rights to underground water, I think at a fourth of the assessed value. Of course, that would stop you from bringing any suit against the City.

D: Were you around for the Alabama Gates incident?

B: I was in Bishop.

D: Were you?

B: I was in Bishop that day and the town was pretty deserted. All the townspeople were down there; it wasn't the farmers.

D: You say the farmers were there?

B: No!

D: You said that you were the county assessor. Can you tell me about your job as assessor?

B: First, I was superintendent of schools and I took the wrong attitude in regard to the power of publicity, and was defeated. But the board of supervisors, then appointed me county assessor and I held out for six and a half years.

I think the only people left that were actively engaged in that row with the City are Gus Cashbaugh and myself. They are all dead, the rest of them, because that was quite awhile ago. Old Father Time gets you. When I came down here to Independence I think there were 36 pupils and one teacher. They are all dead now, but four, and here I am kicking around yet. [laughter]

D: Apparently, some of the farmers started forming irrigation pools.

B: The Bishop Creek Ditch Company was the first pool that I knew of. Cashbaugh was one of them and I was one of them, and Jones the assessor was one of them. That's when we went to Los Angeles to sell out and that Owens Valley Protective Association held a meeting and they were going to stop us from coming back.

D: While we are speaking about this, Miss Enid Larson mentioned that you had to protect her father at one time.

B: Yeah. Her father, well, he didn't belong to the Glasscock outfit. He lived out there in the Sunland country and Cashbaugh and I and somebody else went out there to see him. He told us, "Don't come back anymore because they are watching you." When the Irrigation District was being formed, they had a lawyer who came from Merced. One day I was walking along the street in Bishop, and he gave me a sign. We were going up the stairs of a two-story building and he said, "You and Gus Cashbaugh and Tom Williams keep your mouths shut, there are a lot of people laying to hear what you say." That's the kind of mess we were in all the time.

D: I've read about the Klan activities.

B: I think it was a club of some kind, but I don't know much about them.

D: Mr. Cashbaugh mentioned one time that he was invited to a Klan meeting out at the fairgrounds. Did you know anything about that?

B: Only what he told me. I wasn't invited to any meetings.

D: Well, apparently that turned out to be where they were warning him or something like that.

B: After the banks failed, Walter Young, one of Watterson's right hand supporters came to me and said there was going to be a meeting up there. So, they held a meeting at the Watterson's and it was decided that the city of Los Angeles was to blame, and the city of Los Angeles was to pay. Nobody realized what a hole the bank was in until long after [the banks closed]. I suppose there is a lot of stuff that I could remember, but I can't recall it right now.

D: I guess the Wattersons had quite a bit of land, didn't they?

B: Oh yeah. I think it was controlled by what they called Watterson Brothers, Inc. Of course, Wilfred was the chairman, and he ran the thing. They sold that for $350,000 and nobody knew where the money went.

D: How did they justify that [selling their ranch] to the people?

B: I don't know. It's like one fellow of Big Pine that I talked to. He had been a big supporter of the Wattersons, too, and these things commenced to showing up. He said, "I went up to Bishop to have these things explained to me and they told one lie to cover up another." I often wondered, they must have been in an awful fix because they knew the end was coming.

I got the last payment [for my ranch] from the City on the 28th of July; I put it in the bank and the bank blew up on the 7th of August. I lost $18,000.

D: I guess some people lost every cent they ever had.

B: One old fellow out here, Paul Zucco, an Italian, had accumulated property and sold it to the City for more than $90,000. He owed the bank some money. He cancelled the debt that he had, and deposited the rest to his credit. When the blowup came, he still owed $90,000 and his debts were not paid.

D: Even though he put $90,000 in the bank?

B: Yeah. I guess he would have finished the Wattersons if somebody hadn't found him in Bishop and knew what he was doing. He was waiting for them.

My wife's sister's husband was a cashier in the bank here. He didn't know what was going on. There was a fellow here [by the name of] Stokes who had sold a little piece of ground to the City and had the money in the bank. The bank failed and he laid all the failure on to Pete Mairs, my brother-in-law. He [Stokes] had killed a man in Kernville before that. They found him in the courthouse waiting for Pete. They got him [Stokes] out of there. It's a wonder somebody wasn't killed.

D: You mentioned in your article that somebody did commit suicide.

B: Yeah, Joe Garner. He was slipping quickly, I know now. He came to me one time and wanted to see the City people. I didn't know what he wanted [with the City] but he was a fine fellow, a good man. So, I came with him down here. Later on, he went back and got it into his head that people had it in for him.

D: You mentioned that he slept in an empty silo.

B: He slept outside, I think, in a silo.

D: Because he felt that he needed protection?

B: Yes, it was for protection. He expected somebody would come after him. It was an uncomfortable feeling because you never knew when someone [might come after you], after taking Hall out the way they did. They had told George Watterson to get out. You were watched all the time.

People down here [Independence] didn't have all that trouble. That's another thing. This country here had practically been wiped out by Rickey, the cattle man. He had bought up all the land from here to Big Pine. Fred Eaton bought him out first.

D: Oh, I hadn't heard about that.

B: Yeah.

D: Eaton bought him out when they were planning for the aqueduct?

B: When the City first commenced buying. I think he held to the thought that he was going to have a big cattle ranch. [Eaton] was buying land for the city of Los Angeles. But I don't know, he got several thousand head of cattle in the mix-up someway or another.

D: Who did you say he [Eaton] had bought out?

B: Rickey?

D: No, Eaton.

B: Rickey owned land in Long Valley too, a big cattle outfit, and sold that to Eaton also. Rickey afterwards went to spreading out in other things and went broke. My father knew the Rickeys when they were just kids. They were about his age. One of them was staying all night with him one time. My father asked him, "Does your father know you are here?" "No," he said, "he don't know." My father said, "Won't he get after you for it?" He said, "I'll take care of the old son-of-a-bitch and he won't get hold of me." [laughter]

D: I read in one of the books about Major C. P. Watson.

B: Major Watson? He was a dynamite expert.

D: That's what they say in the literature. Did you know him personally?

B: I knew him personally, yeah.

D: The literature accused him of doing quite a bit of the dynamiting. Do you think maybe he was the one who was doing a lot of it?

B: He had been a major in the Army. Incidentally, he was a Seneca Indian. He didn't look it, but he told me he was. I think he was the one that engineered the dynamiting, yeah. He was one of the local bunch of radicals. I think they found some dynamite in his car.

D: After the banks failed, I guess a lot of people were forced to leave the Valley.

B: Well, they had sold their ranches, had a lot of money, and were moving anyhow.

D: When the banks failed, was that the end of most of the trouble?

B: Yes, the Wattersons were in back of the whole business.

D: According to one of the books I have read it said that L. C. Hall was successful in securing most of the water rights; was it on the McNally Ditch?

B: Yeah, it was the McNally Ditch. I don't know if he was successful in securing the water rights. He helped all the farmers out.

D: He was helping the farmers. It is also said that the farmers could not get loans in the Valley.

B: Well, I know when we built this house in 1937, the bank wouldn't loan us the money. I had a brother-in-law who worked for the Occidental Life Insurance Company, and he could get it there. When the bank here found out, they gave us surplus money to build this.

D: Did you ever hear of any of the farmers bringing suit against the City?

B: Yeah. It got to be kind of a racket even before they ever started pumping. I had an uncle who had a homestead in the foothills west of Bishop. You couldn't have pumped water there in a thousand years. He got quite a bit of money, too, to stop the lawsuit.

D: Do you think a lot of the suits were brought on by selfishness then?

B: Sure, they were. They could get a good price for what they had, and they were glad to get it.

D: Do you think the seizure of the Alabama Gates helped the cause any?

B: No. It got the City into buying out some more land. That's what that dynamiting of the aqueduct was all about. It forced the City to buy some more land. It wasn't to stop the City. Of course they wouldn't say that, but Cashbaugh would tell you the same thing. Some of them did ask outrageous prices.

D: I've read that the City sent out a lot of armed guards or detectives.

B: They had a constable in Lone Pine. Dan Nicoll and Allie McDonald were the deputy sheriffs here. They had those two. They had some spies out, too, but I don't know who they were. There was one around Bishop and every time the farmers held a meeting he was there. We couldn't pin anything on him about being a spy, but that is what he was all right.

D: Did the people know this person was a spy?

B: I knew, but a whole lot of them didn't. I have forgotten now. McDonald and Nicoll were respectable and the City had them for guards.

D: I see. One account said that these guards were armed with tommy guns.

B: I never heard that.

D: It [the article] said they were armed with "Winchesters and tommy guns."

B: They might of had Winchesters. Of course, anything that Glasscock said, you would take with a grain of salt.

D: The tape was off momentarily, and Mr. Brierly was telling me that George Warren was an outspoken man.

B: He was a very outspoken man. He never covered up his actions or thoughts in any way. I stopped at his house north of Big Pine to visit with him. He was there with a six shooter buckled on him, and Sam McMurray, a farmer, was there with a rifle. He said there were several men hidden in the rocks up above to protect him, in case anybody came there to take him away.

He was a director of the Irrigation District, too. He didn't always do what the Irrigation District wanted. I went to their meetings. There was a young woman secretary there, and she got so hot and nervous that she shook like she had a fever.

That Irrigation District was split into certain districts. The people under the Bishop Creek Ditch selected a man named George Clarke. When the election came, the George Clarke name wasn't even mentioned. They had Lawrence Bodle's name on there. Bodle traveled with the other crowd for a little while. Finally, he switched over to George Warren.

D: How did the Keoughs fit in?

B: Well, I don't know what was in back of it. I remember one time they had a meeting up there and Mark Watterson called him out of the room and when he came back he was talking altogether different from the way he was talking before. He was a Watterson supporter.

D: In the 1920s, it was told that the City began increasing groundwater pumping in the Valley and it may have caused some drying up of the lands, and affected some of the existing farmers.

B: I know here in town east of Independence, it used to be called the Spring Field.

It was sub-irrigated ground with springs coming into it. When the City commenced pumping, it dried up. There is no question that when they pump all the water out of here, it is going to dry the country up.

D: Do you remember when the San Francisquito Dam failed? [This is Mr. Delameter speaking. In actuality, it was the Saint Francis Dam in San Francisquito Canyon.]

B: Yes.

D: What was the local reaction to that?

B: I don't know. The day before it happened I went to see H.A. Van Norman about something or other. He talked to somebody over the phone and I knew they were talking about that dam.

I was going to tell you a story here. It doesn't have much to do with the dam, but there was a Tom Coates from Bishop who was working below the St. Francis Dam. Well, after the dam went out, his folks never heard of him. They thought he was dead. After three or four years, we saw a man out there at Fish Springs who had money to buy dogs. I asked somebody, "Who is that chap?" "Well," they said, "that is Tom Coates and he says he knows you." He had a brother in Bishop and he said he thought Tom was dead. I wish I could remember what I was going to tell you, but it skipped my mind. I believe I am getting old. [laughter]

D: The City bought Eaton's property in 1932 to construct the Long Valley Dam.

B: Well, I don't know. I never heard anything about it. I know that he was the fellow in back of that 150-foot dam. If they had built a 150-foot dam in Long Valley, the City would have had to buy his land.

D: Do you think that was the only reason they were pushing for the 150-foot dam?

B: I've heard since then that he owed Inyo County Bank a lot of money, and that if he could get the 150-foot dam and sell his land accordingly, he could pay the bank off.

You know, this mountain land wasn't worth much 45 years ago. I've got 480 acres out there southwest of Bishop I bought for $10 an acre. That was in 1929, when I bought it.

D: I guess it was in the 1930s when Father John Crowley came into the Valley. Did you know him?

B: I knew him to see him, but I never talked with him.

D: They give him a lot of credit for getting tourism going here in the Valley.

B: I think they gave him a lot of credit for something he never did.

D: When the second aqueduct came, was there a lot of opposition to its construction?

B: I don't remember there being any opposition.

D: I just asked Mr. Brierly how he felt about Inyo County's suit against the City over increased groundwater pumping.

B: Well, I had a report one time, and I forgot who made it, but it disappeared. He made a study of this underground water here, and went on to say that there was very little evaporation from more than ten feet down; and there was very little water that ever percolated more than ten feet down. So, water that was pumped out of here would be gone for good, because it would be an accumulation of hundreds of thousands of years. Once pumped out, it is gone.

D: Who made that statement?

B: I don't know. I had a report and lost it, or somebody stole it.

D: Recently, I understand, there was an incident where someone damaged the aqueduct to let water into Diaz Lake. Did you hear about that?

B: Yeah, I heard about that.

D: What do you think about that?

B: Well, they had no authority to do it. Diaz Lake is a bypass for surplus water and it has grown to be quite a resort. Of course, there wasn't much water getting in there, and the lake would get lower and lower. Somebody raised the gate, let the water run in and filled it up. Incidentally, they tell you that Diaz Lake was formed as a result of the earthquake of 1872. I had an uncle who camped there in 1859, and there was a lake there then.

D: That is before the earthquake.

B: Yeah, before the earthquake. It is probably an earthquake fault thousands of years old.

D: Do you think the City has been a good manager of their water and their land here in the Valley?

B: They don't manage the land; they rent it to somebody, and as far as I know, they never pay any attention to it. They figure you are allowed so much water, and then they shut it off.

D: Someone told me that after the City bought up the land, there was a lot of nighttime activity with burning houses.

B: Yeah, I remember that. I think that somebody set fire to the deserted houses.

D: Do you think it was the [previous] owners that were doing it?

B: No, it was probably some of these folks that didn't have any responsibility one way or another, and maybe they would then blame it onto the City.

D: It sounds like maybe a lot of things were laid onto the City that might not have been true.

B: Sure.

D: I just recently read that the City is now attempting to meter everybody in the Valley.

B: They've installed them, but they haven't made any charge yet.

D: A lot of people are very bitter about that.

B: Well, I don't blame the City for being bitter, they turn the water on these lots and let it run for two or three days.

D: Here in the Valley?

B: Yeah. In fact, we've got one out here. These folks next door had somebody turn the water on, and it ran night and day for I don't know how long. If they put a meter on, they wouldn't do it. Of course, a lot depends on how much you are going to charge for the water.

D: Right. No rates have been established yet?

B: No, there has been some talk—just scuttle-butt—same rates they are paying in Los Angeles, but I don't think that's exactly fair. The water only has to come a little way here, but there is nothing definite.

D: Have you ever thought about what the Valley would be like if the City hadn't come in and bought up the land?

B: Well, I have thought about it, but it is a dream, and nobody knows. If they had approved the reclamation project it would have been different, unless the City owned the water.

Wherever the people are, that is where the water is going. I have often thought that about the cattle business, too. When the people move in, the cattle move out. When the City bought up the land, the people moved out, and the cattle moved in. I've got quite a lot of land rented up there around Bishop, and quite a lot of cattle. No, when it comes to telling what it would have been, that's all guesswork.

D: Do you have any feelings toward the environmentalists that you hear about, or the environmental movement in the Valley?

B: Well, I think sometimes they are as bad as the City. There are elk up at Bishop. They are not a native animal, they are imported, and they pay no attention to fences. You can't fence them in, and you can't fence them out. That land that I have up there; the elk tear down the fences, and the cattle get out on the highway. If somebody happens to run into them, who is to blame?

D: We are going to go back here, for just a minute and talk about Sheriff Collins.

B: He was a big, tall, and well-built man, and the expression on his face commanded respect. He was a man that was courageous, too. One time in Big Pine, he had to go upstairs in the hotel to get a man. He went up there and the man pulled a gun on him. Collins said, "Now you can shoot me if you want to, but you will be in more trouble. Now lay down that gun, and come with me." The fellow went with him.

When I first came here, there was a young man who drove the horses up and down the street. He would have a few drinks, and run them. He left and the news came back that he had killed a man somewhere. I don't know about that. He got to thinking that he was a bad man, and when he got back to Darwin, he was out there one night, had a long knife, and was flourishing it around. Collins told him, "You had better put that knife away before somebody gets hurt." Well, this fellow said, "There isn't a man in Inyo County that could make me put this knife away." Well that settled that, Collins took the knife away from him.

I don't know, he had insight into what a fellow had done, and could talk to them, and they would open up and tell a whole lot of stuff.

D: In the article about the Alabama Gates incident, it told about how he wanted the governor to send out the state militia.

B: He was sheriff several times, and the time of that incident, he was against the publicity of Glasscock.* The governor wrote back and said to get them off himself. Collins was a good sheriff. Funny thing, though, he was elected four years and defeated, then elected another four years and defeated. After an election was over, he commenced to working on the people that he knew who were against him, so it would be all right next time.

D: Mr. Brierly, I don't think we got on tape your career here in the Owens Valley. I don't think we talked about all the offices you held. Did we? Would you mention that for me?

B: [laughter] Well, you can look up there.

D: [reading from a wall plaque] It says, "County of Inyo desires to express our sincere appreciation to A. A. Brierly for his excellent and untiring services rendered from 1905 to 1970." That is quite an honor.

B: Yes, it is. They wrote a little article in the paper about me, too. I was probation officer here for a while, too. I have been pretty near everything.

---

* In other words, he was against what Glasscock was publishing in the paper.

D: You retired after that?

B: Yeah, I quit. It got so my legs wouldn't work. I think my mind is all right, but your mind gets to slipping and you don't know it.

D: [laughter] I believe you are doing all right. Mr. Brierly, I have taken a good deal of your time this morning, and I certainly appreciate your allowing me to come in and do this interview.

B: Well, that is all right. I was glad to talk with you.

D: Thank you very much.

END OF INTERVIEW

Author's Note: I believe that when the interview and my 1974 high school paper are examined that one can conclude several things. First, DWP is not the villain it is often portrayed to be. Second, local businessmen were the group responsible for much of the agitation during the land purchase years. Third, many farmers were glad to sell their farms and ranches.

Additionally, I believe that the DWP land purchases have protected, rather than destroyed, the Owens Valley. Without a doubt, the information presented by my grandfather should cause people to wonder about the popular story of DWP as the evil land-robber.

Owens Lake Dust

Much has been made by the Owens Valley radio, television, and print press about DWP's failure to address the problem of dust produced off the lake. Recent events have shown that DWP is making a significant financial contribution to dust mitigation.

Even with DWP's commitment to control the dust on the Lake, there appears to be continued condemnation of DWP for its responsibility for the dust off the Owens Dry Lake. Some individuals seek to blame the DWP for the dust production. Historical record shows that dust has been a problem on Owens Lake and in the Valley since the 1800s. Consider that water diversions from Owens River began many years before DWP's presence in the Valley. DWP is not the sole cause of Owens Lake dry-up!

When I used to listen to my grandfather or other old-timers, they all talked about the dust off the lake and in the Valley. Often these discussions were about a time prior to DWP land ownership in the Valley. I offer the following from my great-great-grandfather, Hugh Enloe's, diary (Enloe, 1891-1893).

On October 23, 1892, he wrote:

It is cloudy in spots with spots of bright sunshine later wind rises from Coyote* violently bringing dust and gloom.

From the *Inyo Independent* newspaper the following were obtained (Babb, personal communication):

October 14, 1871 — An unusually high wind blew from the north night before last. Ordinary houses afforded no protection whatever from the clouds of dust and sand, and the result was to make every body uncommonly "gritty."

April 5, 1873 — Wednesday evening last old Boreas blew down from the western mountain range at a most terrific rate. He came in gusts and left in dust, paper, rags, cans, shingles, and various other things.

April 5, 1873 — [letter to editor] From 2 o'clock to 8 PM yesterday, the most terrific sand and wind storm raged here that has ever been my misfortune to witness. My carpenter got through his job on my house, a 20 x 12 foot shed roof, and in less than three hours it was a bottom side up wreck. Damage is 300 dollars and over. Goodale's new house at Fish Springs which he boasted as being nearly air tight, was besmeared with dust through and through.... D.B. Curtis April 3, 1873.

October 18, 1873 — The four winds all joined forces on the day proceeding the election, and

---

* Coyote refers to Coyote Valley southwest of Bishop.

taking the North Pole for a starting point, came on a howling. People's eyes were filled with dust and their mouths with words the same as ministers use but differently arranged and accented.

April 11, 1874 — Last night we were favored with a howling wind from the south and plenty of dust everywhere.

January 16, 1875 — A little before noon Thursday last old Boreas blew a little blast right out of Kearsarge Canyon, as fresh and strong and dusty as is often witnessed in these quiet latitudes. It never stopped to take a breath or fresh hold for 4 hours. Then it wound up long enough to give over particular people a chance to get dust and sand out of their houses and eyes, then went at it again with slightly diminished force till it got a mild rainstorm fairly started.

April 22, 1876 — Last Tuesday about noon, this place [Independence] was shut out from the sunlight by clouds of dust and sand which swept in masses down the Valley before the wind.

September 26, 1889 — The wind blew fresh and strong all day from the north and dust flew promiscuously.

This is just a sampling of reported dust storms. It appears that dust was a problem long before DWP entered the picture. One source of dust that is not much of a problem in contemporary times, that did exist in the past, was the dust blowing from farmers' fields.

The Owens Valley press and politicians often state that dust [reported as PM-10 levels] off the Owens Lake is the single worst source in the United States. This myth is often reported in large newspapers (*Los Angeles Times*, July 16, 1998). The problem is that no scientific studies have been conducted to support this claim. The press often states that this fact is a direct quote from the Environmental Protection Agency (EPA). I contacted the EPA and obtained PM-10 particulate records for the entire United States for the last six years (EPA Report).

Several points are important. The EPA records PM-10 levels in several ways: first, the highest twenty-four-hour recorded dust production; second, the number of measured days per year that dust standards were exceeded; and third, an estimate of the total number of days that would exceed the standard if observations were taken every day. PM-10 levels are not measured the same number of times per year or per location, therefore the EPA estimates the number of days that the dust levels might be exceeded based on the number of measured days per number of observations.

Table 1 summarizes the PM-10 levels in Inyo County for nine sites from 1992–1997. Not all sites have records for all years. Column 1 lists the site area; column 2 is the site address; column 3 is the maximum recorded twenty-four-hour level in micro grams per cubic meter [$\mu g/m^3$]; column 4 is the average twenty-four-hour level, over the record history for the site; column 5 is the most days in any given year for a site that the PM-10 standards were exceeded; column 6

Table 1. PM-10 Levels Inyo County, California Monitoring Sites

Site	Address	Max 24 hour (µg/cubic meter)	Average 24 hour (µg/cubic meter)	Maximum number of days measured value exceeded standard per year	Average number of days measured value exceeded standard of years of record	Maximum estimated number of days exceeded standard	Years of measurement at site
Lone Pine	Locust Street	133	50	1	1	6	92-97
Olancha	Hwy. 395	366	366	1	1	6	92
Olancha	Fall Road	365	210	1	1	2	94-95
Bishop	Main Street	79	57	0	0	0	94-97
Pearsonville	Pearson Road	392	213	1	1	2.5	94-96
Coso Junction	Hwy. 395	692	164	2	0.5	2	92-97
Coso Junction	10 Miles east of Coso Junction	567	129	2	0.33	2	92-97
Keeler	Railroad Road	781	474	3	1	8	02-94
Keeler	Cerro Gordo Road	2,668	537	5	2.5	10	94-97

is the average number of days the standard was exceeded for the record history; column 7 is the estimated number of days the standard might have been exceeded had observations been taken daily; and column 8 is the years of record for the site.

What is interesting to note is that, while the highest 24-hour recording in the United States was taken at Keeler [2,668 μg/m³, an extreme and unusual event*], the total highest number of days that the standard was exceeded in a given year [per site] in Inyo County ranged from 0 to 5 days per year. More important is that the average number of days per year exceeding the standard at each site in Inyo County, ranged from 0 to 2.5 days over the 1992–1997 period. Therefore, there are very few days per year that air quality is poor in Inyo County, including Keeler (EPA Report).

Maximum values for twenty-four-hour readings in other areas in the U.S include: 1,712 μg/m³ (West Plains, Missouri), 803 μg/m³ (Spokane, Washington), 649 μg/m³ (San Bernardino, California), 587 μg/m³ (Philadelphia, Pennsylvania), 592 μg/m³ (Post Falls, Idaho), 494 μg/m³ (Bay City, Michigan), 480 μg/m³ (Phoenix, Arizona), 441 μg/m³ (Calexico, California), 395 μg/m³ (El Centro, California), 386 μg/m³ (Henderson, Nevada), 339 μg/m³ (Las Vegas, Nevada), and 266 μg/m³ (Teller County, Colorado) (EPA Report). Several of these sites are near industrial centers, others are natural dust producers, some are influenced by agriculture.

---

* Dust concentrations are presented in metric format. However, to give an example in English units the 2,668 micro grams per cubic meter (μg/m³) = .000003 ounces per cubic foot (oz/ft³).

An average of all maximum records for all sites for all the years of record from 1992–1997 in Inyo County gives a 160 μg/m³ yearly maximum twenty-four-hour reading; in other words, lower than many sites in the rest of the U.S.

Taking the analysis one step further: The maximum number of days in Inyo County measured per year exceeding the EPA PM-10 standard (for all Inyo County sites) is 2.5 days (1992-1997), with an estimated number of days exceeding the standard of 108. Compare that with other areas' yearly (maximum on record 1992-1997) number of days exceeding the standard: Calexico, California–7 days measured exceeding the standard, 42 days estimated; Phoenix, Arizona–25 days measured exceeding the standard and 365 days estimated (only 25 actual observations, i.e., all measured days exceeded the standard); Lewiston, Idaho–20 days measured exceeding the standard and over 100 estimated; Las Vegas, Nevada–5 days measured exceeding the standard and 10 days estimated (EPA Report).

The maximum twenty-four-hour and number of days per year exceeding the standard may vary wildly at the same monitoring site by year. These figures above are illustrations of maximum values per site for the 1992–1997 record.

So, while Owens Lake may have the highest twenty-four-hour record, it IS NOT THE WORST area in the U.S. for PM-10 levels on a per day basis (natural or otherwise), which in my view may be the more important variable of concern.

It must also be realized that many lacustrine sites have no PM-10 monitoring near them. If one travels across the Great Basin through the old dry lake deposits, dust storms aplenty may be encountered. Since these areas are remote, there are no monitoring sites located near them, and therefore, we have no idea what the PM-10 levels are. Thereby, the statements about Owens Lake producing the worst dust in the U.S. are misleading and slanted.

This misrepresentation of facts is one more example of how individuals seek to promote their own agendas [blame DWP for everything] with total disregard for the truth. It is a sad state of affairs. I hope my presentation of this information enlightens the unenlightened.

I realize that the EPA requires bringing the dust levels under the standard. I also believe that the dust is not healthy for those who live directly in the path of the storms. However, DWP will spend millions for solving a problem that is not wholly their responsibility (remember farmers diverted water prior to land acquisition by DWP). It also seems that the "crisis" to fix the dust problem has been overstated and may not need the immediate attention some Owens Valley residents have been led to believe.

Some final thoughts regarding the dust should be considered. First, if ranchers had maintained the ownership in the Valley and they had dried up the Owens Lake, as surely would have occurred, would they be held to the same standard for dust mitigation as DWP? I think not. It appears that when environmentalists look for a target they often pick a government source. When government agencies (such as DWP) are forced to mitigate environmental problems, in the long run it is the citizens who pay the bill. Second, I am much more disturbed by the smog rolling into the Valley throughout the summer as well as the winter fireplace and wood stove smoke hanging in the Valley than I am by occasional dust storms. Yet, few individuals seem to be as indignant about the smog and smoke problem as they are about dust. Is that because to mitigate these two air pollutants requires personal sacrifice? I wonder. If you doubt that the Valley has a smog problem, just climb to the summit of any of the surrounding mountain peaks and look at the "haze" in the Valley. Or better yet, go up in a small airplane and fly over any part of the Great Basin or Southwest. The entire region is often inundated with smog. Again, few people seem to care.

This chapter illustrates once more how the truth is not fully described where issues regarding DWP are concerned. Let us hope that the solutions to the Lake dust problem actually work and that the millions of dollars to be spent on control are not thrown away.

The Valley, As I See It

The current political climate seems to dictate that DWP be chastised for all its land management decisions in the Valley. Additionally, it appears to me that many groups and individuals seek to have DWP release land for development, and wish to create more jobs, promote industry, condemn livestock grazing, and cry foul for every practice DWP has undertaken. To these individuals and groups I say, be careful of what you ask for, you may get it! I believe that residential and industrial (light or otherwise) development would lead to the destruction of one of the greatest and most unique areas left in the country.

DWP's presence in the Valley has maintained open spaces for everyone to use and enjoy. We have all come to expect that this is the way it should be, that we have the right to go where we want and do almost anything we want within the Valley. This "right" is, in fact, a privilege that should be cherished. DWP has made this freedom of movement possible. Travel to any other region where there are open spaces and see how different land use is in those areas. Private land owners are not as open to public use as is DWP.

DWP land holdings have kept development in Owens Valley to a minimum. We should all be grateful! Development becomes a cancer on the landscape as prime open space is divided into "ranchettes" and subdivisions. Industrial complexes, whether light or otherwise, surround the communities and destroy the small-town atmosphere of once rural communities.

For anyone doubting what devastation development can bestow on scenic rural areas, I suggest they review *National Geographic*'s article "Colorado's Front Range" (Long, Nov. 1996). Having lived in that region of Colorado for four years, I have seen firsthand the destruction of development on rural landscapes. There is a strong movement in many towns in the Colorado Front Range area to stop or, at a minimum, slow growth so the rural life style will continue. I am thankful that presently Owens Valley residents don't have to contend with the problems development has caused Colorado's Front Range. However, I believe that the same negative impacts would occur here if too much land were released by DWP, and second, I'm sure that had DWP not purchased all the land, this Valley would be very much like the Colorado Front Range. That is to say, overcrowded with congested roads, piecemeal land development, smoggy skies and, in fact, an urban setting in a scenic landscape.

Land releases under the DWP-Inyo County Memorandum of Understanding (MOU) must be managed with care. I believe the majority of Owens Valley residents do not wish to lose their rural life styles. I hope the political planners don't allow much development. I would much rather see a few homes with larger lots (one acre minimum) and more park areas that utilize the newly released lands. Only time will tell what will actually transpire.

Another issue that concerns me, and in my opinion needs to be addressed, is the contention that the Owens Valley once possessed green grasslands and vast farmlands prior to DWP water diversions. Somewhere, the idea that this area was a farming mecca has become fact. In reality, the Owens Valley green belt scenario just isn't true. While there was a short history of farming and ranching, the period was, at the same time, marred by difficulty. Most of the farms in the region were, at best, subsistence operations. Families eked out a living. There were struggles over water long before DWP arrived, as noted by my great-great-grandfather Hugh S. Enloe. (Enloe diary, May 16, 1892). "I rise late and cook breakfast and then turn a full head* on the middle of the alfalfa and come back and the gate [irrigation] was lowered several inches and Mr. McCloud came galloping up and explained matters and said that Mr. Rawson and others had scarcely any water and that he would have to shut down our gates to the amount of water each individual owned. I told him that I did not use the water half the time but that he was the authority and go ahead and do what he thought was right and I would do the same." (May 19, 1892) "Mr. Watson's Indian takes a tremendous head of water so I am not using any till I see what the water boss says or does."

As my grandfather told me, many farmers were glad to have DWP buy their lands because they were not able to make a decent living. Consider the differ-

---

* A "full head" refers to the maximum amount of irrigation water he could obtain.

ences in the Valley if farming had prevailed. The land would not be open for the public to enjoy, and like many other once scenic agricultural areas in California, this area would be vastly developed. While this is only my opinion, I am sure, with the close proximity to Los Angeles, that the Owens Valley would be extensively developed had not the DWP purchased the land.

Also, the view that DWP has created a desert in the region is false. Natural mean rainfall in the Valley is slightly over five inches per year. That limited rainfall produces a desert by itself. Runoff from the Sierra and Owens River flooding in the springtime did produce wetland areas that no longer exist. However, as a whole, these were small acreages when compared to the entire Valley. William Irelan (Eighth Annual Report, 1888), describing his trip through the region in 1870 as State Mineralogist, wrote, "...the east side of the Owens River is a country which is practically an unbroken desert as no streams of any considerable magnitude issue from either the Inyo or White Mountains." He described the Valley floor as "a strip of bottom land, varying from one to two or three miles in width, [which] borders the river throughout the Valley.... The soil of this bottom land is generally good, and it is covered with grass, affording feed for considerable herds of cattle and horses, which are driven here at times from the San Joaquin Valley.... The feed is generally, however, rather coarse.... Skirting the edge of this bottom land, and between it and the foot of the mountains proper, on either side of the Valley are sagebrush slopes, consisting of the wash from the mountains." He goes on to mention the "beautiful" streams which flow over the wash from the Sierra to Owens River. Nowhere does he mention grasslands other than the river region and areas near the stream flowing from the Sierras. This is how my grandfather remembered the Valley, too. Additionally, farming was primarily confined to the area around Bishop in the late 1800s.

The Valley has no doubt changed. The Owens Lake was surely drained by the water diversions (first by Valley farmers and then by DWP), the Valley water table has lowered, and native plant communities have no doubt suffered. However, my view is that when evaluating all the pros and cons of the water diversions and DWP-owned lands, we are all better off with the current situation. We can address the environmental issues, but let us not jump to change the status quo of land management by DWP.

The importance of today's ranching community in preserving Owens Valley must not be overlooked either. Most of the green meadow areas in the Valley are a result of irrigation. These areas provide not only forage for livestock, but also support a wide variety of wildlife. Without ranchers to irrigate these meadows there would be less green space than exists today. The cry to remove livestock ranchers from the western desert regions has become a popular chant in recent years. It is another view that should be well thought out before implementation, especially where private lands are involved. Simply put, when ranchers leave, development moves in. In the case of Owens Valley, if ranchers move out, dry lands move in. If DWP sells land, then in comes development.

For those interested in further reading regarding the land purchases in the Owens Valley I recommend reading *The Owens Valley, City of Los Angeles, Water Controversy: An Oral History Examination of the Events of the 1920s and the 1970s*, written by Charles Delameter for his Masters Thesis at California State University, Fullerton. This text is an invaluable source of information. The thesis contains interviews with several individuals (My grandfather, Wilfred Partridge, Mary DeDecker, Omie Mairs, et. al) regarding the DWP and their activities. Mr. Delameter summarizes the issues between DWP and Owens Valley residents in the 1920s and 1970s, and then makes some conclusions about land purchases by DWP. I don't agree with all his views, but it is a well-researched document worth reading. Another scholarly work is *Los Angeles and the Owens River Aqueduct* by Gordon Miller, Doctoral Dissertation, Claremont Graduate School. This is a well researched document. Finally, *Vision or Villainy* by Abraham Hoffman (Hoffman, 1981) presents a fair evaluation of the controversy.

In the *Water Seekers*, Remi Nadeau states the following: "At some time in the dim future, might not Inyo County decide to invoke the public trust doctrine [as was done at Mono Lake]? And might it then reach for the vision of a well-rounded and self-sufficient community that it shared with the Reclamation Service back in 1903?" (Nadeau, 1997). He suggests that Owens Valley residents might take up the same cause as the Mono Lake Committee to keep water in the Owens Valley and refill Owens Lake, yet in another section of the book he notes that where the water goes, comes pollution, crowding, and all the other negative aspects of development. In contrast to people like Mr. Nadeau, I believe we are lucky to live where we do, and to have DWP own and manage the lands.

As Gordon Miller wrote in his dissertation in reference to the possibilities of tourism and recreation, "the Valley's economic prospects were brighter than they ever could have been had it remained strictly a farming community" (Miller, 1978). It is the open lands and access to them for the general public which makes this, the Owens Valley region, unique. We must not forget that.

I hope I have inspired those who criticize DWP to see my perspective on the water and land issues. Many in the Valley feel as I do. I believe we are the silent majority. I know deep within my heart, and from my study of facts, that the citizenry of the Valley is far better off with the presence of DWP than without it.

I was blessed to have the influence and counsel of my grandfather. He spoke the truth about the early times involving DWP and the Owens Valley because he lived them. He wasn't passing on diluted and distorted stories from others. I miss his company and intelligence. He taught me much, from simple things like how to carve a whistle from a willow stem (as taught to him by *his* grandfather) to the importance of education, reading, and learning. He often said small minds talk about people, average minds talk about things, great minds speak about ideas. His life was extraordinary in many ways. It was people like him and his friends who truly knew the Valley. These old-timers are now all gone. I believe what is presented in this paper would please him.

Some might ask why I wrote this book in the presence of several positive agreements between Inyo County and DWP after a history of litigation. First, I wish for a more balanced reporting of land purchases by DWP in the early part of the century. Second, I fear, as DWP loses control over their lands (through increased pressure from litigation) in the Valley and Mono Basin, that they may consider releasing more land. It is my view that the influence of environmental groups (such as the Sierra Club, et. al) on land management decisions will be in many instances detrimental as opposed to beneficial to the Valley. If DWP can't use the land, why should they have the tax burden? As the expense of mitigation (such as rewatering the Lower Owens River, dust control on Owens Lake, refilling Mono Lake, etc.) becomes too great, why keep the land? It might be more economically sound to sell land and purchase water elsewhere. If DWP sells land, there will likely be more homes and more people coming to the Valley. Third, I wish to see land management in the Valley carried out in a fair manner for all users and owners (DWP, Inyo County, ranchers, and recreationalists). I am concerned about the apparent increase in influence of environmental groups on DWP land management decisions in the Owens Valley. These groups have no "vested" interest in the Valley as do groups such as ranchers. Yet the views and concerns of environmental groups outweigh the needs of ranchers who have a direct interest in preserving the land. This seems an unfair and unjust way to manage land. I hope DWP will keep their vision and history of land management in the Valley.

As a winter storm blows along the landscape, I drive across the Valley from Big Pine, up Westgard Pass and off on an obscure dirt track. I park my Jeep on a hilltop overlooking "my Valley." I know this is a land worth saving. I hope those who promote development and the removal of the DWP from the Valley look hard and long at their ideas. When all the facts are considered, including evaluating the alternative to DWP land ownership in the Valley, I know the positive value of DWP's presence will be seen. We can wander all over these vast and primitive lands as if they belonged to each and every one of us. It is a privilege we should cherish and protect. Dark clouds hang on the Sierras and a mist still falls from the sky as I close my eyes and wonder, how long will the serenity of the Valley survive?

A.A. Brierly Vitae

Married 1915

Second Marriage December 2, 1931

Inyo County school teacher 1905–1913; 1915-1922

Inyo County Undersheriff 1913–1915

Inyo County Superintendent of Schools 1922–1926

Inyo County Probation Officer 1927

Inyo County Tax Assessor 1928–1934

Inyo County Surveyor 1934–1970

Member Inyo County Board of Education 1920–1922

Member Owens Valley Unified School District Board of Trustees 1956

Special Deputy Sheriff 1913–1982, Inyo County Badge number 127

State Director of California Cattlemen's Association

Selective Service Board, twenty years

Inyo County Planning Commission

Inyo County Democratic Central Committee

Inyo-Mono Counties Coordinating Council

Appraiser for the Bakersfield Production Credit Association

Daughters of the American Revolution Honor Medal
    recipient
Inyo-Mono Cowbelles "Father of the Year" 1970
Memberships:
National Cattlemen's Association
California Cattlemen's Association
Inyo County Cattlemen's Association
Morgan Horse Association
Belgian Horse Association
California Wool Growers Association
California Farm Bureau
Independence Lions Club
Independence Civic Club
Oddfellows Lodge
Cole County Historical Society, Missouri
Cass County Historical Society, Missouri
Missouri Historical Society
California Historical Society
Eastern California Historical Society
American Congress on Surveying and Mapping, life
    member
American Institute of Mining and Metallurgical Engineers

Bibliography

Babb, Dave. Dust storm events recorded in the *Inyo Independent* compilation. Bishop, CA.

Bryant, William Cullen, ed. *A Library of Poetry and Song.* NY, NY: J.B. Ford and Company Publishers. 1871.

Cone, Marla. *Los Angeles Times.* "LA Owens Valley Agree on Plan to Stop Dust Storms." Thursday, July 16, 1998.

Delameter, Charles Ellis. *The Owens Valley, City of Los Angeles, Water Controversy: An Oral History Examination of the Events of the 1920s and the 1970s.* M.S. Thesis. California State University, Fullerton. Fullerton, CA. 1977.

Eighth Annual Report of the State Mineralogist, Year ending October 1, 1888. Sacramento, CA: State Printing, 1888.

Enloe, Hugh S. Diary written from his home in Bishop, CA. December 29, 1891–July 16, 1893.

EPA, Quick Look Report. *EPA Aeromatic Information Retrieval System.* Air Quality Subsystem. State by State Record for the Entire United States.

Franklin, Benjamin. *Essays, Articles, Bagatelles, and Letters. Poor Richard's Almanac. AutoBiography.* J.A. Leo Lemay, Editor. NY, NY: The Library of America, Literary Classics of the United States. 1987.

Hoffman, Abraham. *Vision or Villainy. Origins of the Owens Valley - Los Angeles Water Controversy.* College Station, TX: Texas A & M University Press. 1981.

Long, Michael E. "Colorado's Front Range." *National Geographic.* Vol. 190, No. 5. p. 80 -103. Washington, D.C.: National Geographic Society. Nov. 1996.

Miller, Gordon. "Los Angeles and the Owens River Aqueduct." Ph.D. Dissertation. Claremont Graduate School. 1978.

Nadeau, Remi, *The Water Seekers* 4th ed. Santa Barbara, CA: Crest Publishers. 1997.

About the Author

Robert A. Pearce, born in Bishop, California, is a grandson of Arlie Brierly. Rob spent his youth through high school in the Owens Valley. He graduated from Bishop Union High School in 1974. He then attended California Polytechnic State University, San Luis Obispo, and received a Bachelor of Science degree in Agricultural Management. After college graduation Pearce worked for six summers for Mineral King Pack Station east of Visalia, California. He was a manager at Compston Feedlot in Smith, Nevada, and spent time in Big Timber, Montana, as a ranch hand. In 1983 Pearce returned to Bishop to manage his family's ranch. Unfortunately, the family had to sell the ranch, so in 1985 Robert moved to Texas where he broke colts. He worked for horse trainers in Texas and California for a couple of years. He returned to California and worked for Cal Trans and the Los Angeles Department of Water and Power for short stints. In 1989 he was accepted to Texas A & M University as a Masters degree candidate and graduated in 1991 with a M.S. in Range Science. He continued his education, receiving his Doctorate in Rangeland Ecosystem Science from Colorado State University in 1995. During two summers of his graduate studies he returned to the Owens Valley and worked for the U.S. Forest Service, White Mountain, District as a Range Technician. He was also employed by Inyo County for a year and a half. Rob now lives in Bishop, California, and continues to be involved with natural resource issues in the Owens Valley.